VEDANTA PHILOSOPHY

VEDANTA PHILOSOPHY

F. MAX MULLER

GYAN

Published by

Gyan Publishing House
5, Ansari Road
Daryaganj, New Delhi-110002
Phone: 011-47034999, 9811692060
E-mail: books@gyanbooks.com

Distribution Network
gyanbooks.com
India, USA, Canada, UK, Australia

ISBN: 978-93-6920-299-7 (PB)

First Published, 1950

2nd Impression 2025

Printed at: Gyan Press, Delhi.

VEDANTA PHILOSOPHY
Author: F. MAX MULLER

VEDÂNTA PHILOSOPHY

VEDÂNTA PHILOSOPHY

BY

F. MAX MÜLLER, K.M.

MEMBER OF THE FRENCH INSTITUTE

1894

TABLE OF CONTENTS

FIRST LECTURE.

ORIGIN OF THE VEDÂNTA PHILOSOPHY.

	PAGE
The Importance of Philosophy	1
What is important and what is merely curious . .	2
The Importance of the Vedânta Philosophy . . .	6
Opinions of the Vedânta by Schopenhauer, Sir W. Jones, Victor Cousin, F. Schlegel	8
The Vedânta, both Philosophy and Religion . . .	11
The Upanishads as Vedânta	15
The Four Stages of Life	18
Relation of the Soul (Âtman) to Brahman (the Parama-âtman)	20
Unsystematic Character of the Upanishads . . .	22
Growth of Religious and Philosophic Thought before the Upanishads	25
Belief in one God	27
Two Forms of the Vedânta	29
The Upanishads treated as Revealed, not as Historical Books	32
Moral Preparation for the Study of the Vedânta . .	36
Mistrust in the Evidence of the Senses	40
Metaphorical Language of the Upanishads . . .	42

SECOND LECTURE.

The Soul and God.

PAGE
Extracts from the Upanishads 47
I. From the Ka*th*a Upanishad 47
II. From the Maitrâya*n*a Upanishad . . . 55
*S*a*n*kara's Analysis of Subject and Object . . . 61
The Inheritance of the Vedânta 71
No Esoteric Vedânta 72
Relation between the Higher Bráhman and the Lower Brahmán 82
Relation between the Higher Âtman and the Living Âtman 87
Different Views of the Soul in Indian Philosophy . . 89
The Upâdhis as the cause of difference between the Soul and God 92
The Psychology of the Vedânta 94
Our Mind is not our Self (Âtman) 97
The Upâdhis due to Avidyâ 97
Nescience (Âvidya) destroyed by Knowledge (Vidyâ) . 100
How the Soul can be one with God 102

THIRD LECTURE.

Similarities and Differences between Indian and European Philosophy.

Strangeness of Eastern Philosophy 108
General Interest of Indian Philosophy 110
Critical Treatment of Oriental Literature . . . 112
The Sacred Syllable Om 115
Whatever was Old became Sacred 117

PAGE

Books for the Study of the Vedânta 118
Coincidences. Spinoza's 'Substantia' 123
The Meanings of Real 126
The Nature of Avidyâ and Mâyâ 128
Colebrooke on Mâyâ 129
Sir W. Jones on the Vedânta 131
The Two Brahmans are One 132
The Germs of the Vedânta in the Upanishads . . 135
The Knowledge of Brahman 138
Names and Forms the Objects of Brahmán's Knowledge 140
Thought and Language Inseparable 141
Coincidences between Names and Forms and the Greek Logos 142
Speech as a Creative Power in the Veda 144
Similarity with the Old Testament Wisdom . . . 146
Did Brahman mean Word? 147
Brahman derived from the same Root as *Verbum* and *Word* 149
Names and Forms the Connecting-link between Brahman and the World 151
The Gods of other Religions 154
Names and Forms the Product of Avidyâ . . . 158
The Vedânta in Practical Life 161
The Ethics of the Vedânta 162
The Doctrine of Karman 165
Pre-existence of the Soul 167
Recapitulation 170

THREE INTRODUCTORY LECTURES

ON THE

VEDÂNTA PHILOSOPHY

LECTURE I.

Origin of the Vedânta Philosophy.

The Importance of Philosophy.

I am fully aware of the difficulties which I shall have to encounter in trying to enlist your interest, nay, if possible, your sympathy, for an ancient system of Indian Philosophy, the Vedânta Philosophy. It is no easy task, even within the walls of this scientific Institution, to obtain a hearing for a mere system of philosophy, whether new or old. The world is too busy to listen to purely theoretical speculations; it wants exciting experiments and, if possible, tangible results. And yet I remember one who ought to be well known to all of you in this place, I remember our dear friend Tyndall, rejoicing over a new theory, because, as he said, 'Thank God, it will not produce any practical results; no one will ever be able to take out a patent and make money by it.' Leibniz, I suppose, took no patent for his Differential Calculus, nor Sir Isaac Newton for his theory of gravitation. Trusting in that spirit of Tyndall's, which has been so long the presiding spirit of this busy laboratory of thought, I hope that there may be some friends and admirers of his left within these walls, who are willing to listen to mere speculations,—speculations which will never produce any tangible results, in the ordinary sense of the word, for which certainly no one can take out a patent, or hope, if he had secured it, to make any money by it;—and yet these speculations are bound up with the highest and dearest interests of our life.

What is important and what is merely curious.

The system of philosophy for which I venture to claim your attention is chiefly concerned with the *Soul* and its relation to *God.* It comes to us from India, and is probably more than two thousand years old. Now the soul is not a popular subject in these days. Even if its existence is not denied altogether, it has long been ranged among subjects on which 'it is folly to be wise.' However, if I were to claim your attention for a Greek or German system of philosophy, if I were to tell you what Plato or Kant have said about the soul, it is just possible that their sayings might at least be considered as *curious*. But I must say at once that this would not satisfy me at all. I look upon that word *curious* as a lazy and most objectionable word. If a man says, 'Yes, that is very curious,' what does he mean? What he really means is this,—'Yes, that is very curious, but no more.' But why no more? Not because it is of no importance in itself, but simply because in the pigeon-holes of his own mind, there is no place as yet ready to receive it; simply because the chords of his mind are not attuned to it, and do not vibrate in harmony with it; simply because he has no real sympathy with it. To a well-stored mind and to a well-arranged intellect there ought to be nothing that is simply curious; nay it has been truly said that almost every great discovery, all real progress in human knowledge is due to those who could discover behind what to the world at large seemed merely curious, something really important, something pregnant with results. The electric spark of the lightning has been curious as long as the world exists; it seems but yesterday that it has become really important.

If my object were simply to amuse you I could place before you a very large collection of soul-curios, tell you ever so many curious things about the soul, sayings collected from uncivilized and from civilized races. There are, first of all, the names of the soul, and some of them, no doubt, full of interest. Among the names applied to the soul, some mean breath, others heart, others midriff, others blood, others the pupil of the eye, all showing that they were meant for something connected with the body, something supposed to have its abode in the eye, in the heart, in the blood or the breath, yet different from every one of these coarse material objects. Other names are purely metaphorical, as when the soul was called a bird, not because it was believed to be a bird, caged in the body, but because it seemed winged in its flights of thought and fancy; or when it was called a shadow, not because it was believed to be the actual shadow which the body throws on a wall (though this is held by some philosophers), but because it was *like* a shadow, something perceptible, yet immaterial and not to be grasped. Of course, after the soul had once been likened to and called a shadow, every kind of superstition followed, till people persuaded themselves that a dead body can no longer throw a shadow. Again, when the soul had once been conceived and named, its name, in Greek ψυχή, was transferred to a butterfly, probably because the butterfly emerged winged from the prison of the chrysalis. And here, too, superstition soon stepped in and represented pictorially the soul of the departed as issuing from his mouth in the shape of a butterfly. There is hardly a tribe, however uncivilized and barbarous, which has not a name for soul, that is for something different from the body, yet closely allied to it and hard at work within it. It was but lately that I received from the Bishop of North Caledonia a new metaphor for soul. The Zimshiân Indians have a word which means both soul and fragrance. When questioned by the Bishop on the subject, the Indians replied: 'Is not a man's soul to his body what the fragrance is to the flower?' This, no doubt, is as good a metaphor as any, and it may fairly claim a place by the side of Plato's metaphor in the 'Phaedo,' where he compares the soul to the harmonious music that can be drawn from a lyre.

If I wished to excite your interest in a collection of such curios, I might place before you ever so many names, ever so many metaphors, ever so many sayings with reference to the soul. Nay, if looked upon as contributions to a study of the evolution of the human mind, as documents for the history of human wisdom or human folly, such curious sayings might even claim a certain scientific value, as giving us an insight into the ancient workshop of the human intellect.

The Importance of the Vedânta Philosophy.

But I may say at once that I shall not be satisfied with metaphors, however poetical or beautiful, and that in placing before you an outline of the Vedânta Philosophy I have far higher objects in view. I wish to claim the sympathy not only of your mind, but of your heart for the profoundest thoughts of Indian thinkers about the soul. After all, I doubt whether the soul has really lost with all of us that charm which it exercised on ancient thinkers. We still say, 'What shall it profit a man, if he shall gain the whole world, and lose his own soul?' And how can we even claim to have a soul to lose, if we do not know what we mean by soul. But if it seem strange to you that the old Indian philosophers should have known more about the soul than Greek or Mediaeval or modern philosophers, let us remember that however much the telescopes for observing the stars of heaven have been improved, the observatories of the soul have remained much the same, for I cannot convince myself that the observations now made in the so-called physico-psychological laboratories of Germany, however interesting to physiologists, would have proved of much help to our Vedânta philosophers. The rest and peace which are required for deep thought or for accurate observation of the movements of the soul, were more easily found in the silent forests of India than in the noisy streets of our so-called centres of civilization.

Opinions of the Vedânta by Schopenhauer, Sir W. Jones, Victor Cousin, F. Schlegel.

Anyhow, let me tell you that a philosopher so thoroughly acquainted with all the historical systems of philosophy as Schopenhauer, and certainly not a man given to deal in extravagant praise of any philosophy but his own, delivered his opinion of the Vedânta Philosophy, as contained in the Upanishads, in the following words: 'In the whole world there is no study so beneficial and so elevating as that of the Upanishads. It has been the solace of my life, it will be the solace of my death.' If these words of Schopenhauer's required any endorsement, I should willingly give it as the result of my own experience during a long life devoted to the study of many philosophies and many religions.

If philosophy is meant to be a preparation for a happy death, or Euthanasia, I know of no better preparation for it than the Vedânta Philosophy.

Nor is Schopenhauer by any means the only authority who speaks in such rapturous terms of the ancient philosophy of India, more particularly of the Vedânta Philosophy.

Sir William Jones, no mean authority as an oriental as well as a classical scholar, remarks 'that it is impossible to read the Vedânta or the many fine compositions in illustration of it, without believing that Pythagoras and Plato derived their sublime theories from the same fountain with the sages of India.' (Works, Calcutta ed., i. pp. 20, 125, 127.) It is not quite clear whether Sir William Jones meant that the ancient Greek philosophers borrowed their philosophy from India. If he did, he would find few adherents in our time, because a wider study of mankind has taught us that what was possible in one country, was possible in another also. But the fact remains nevertheless that the similarities between these two streams of philosophical thought in India and in Greece are very startling, nay sometimes most perplexing.

Victor Cousin, the greatest among the historians of philosophy in France, when lecturing at Paris in the years 1828 and 1829 on the history of modern philosophy, before an audience, we are told, of two thousand gentlemen, spoke in the following terms: 'When we read with attention the poetical and philosophical monuments of the East, above all, those of India which are beginning to spread in Europe, we discover there many a truth, and truths so profound, and which make such a contrast with the meanness of the results at which the European genius has sometimes stopped, that we are constrained to bend the knee before the philosophy of the East, and to see in this cradle of the human race the native land of the highest philosophy.' (Vol. i. p. 32.)

German philosophers have always been the most ardent admirers of Sanskrit literature, and more particularly, of Sanskrit philosophy. One of the earliest students of Sanskrit, the true discoverer of the existence of an Indo-European family of speech, Frederick Schlegel, in his work on Indian Language, Literature, and Philosophy (p. 471), remarks: 'It cannot be denied that the early Indians possessed a knowledge of the true God; all their writings are replete with sentiments and expressions, noble, clear, and severely grand, as deeply conceived and reverentially expressed as in any human language in which men have spoken of their God.' And again: 'Even the loftiest philosophy of the Europeans, the idealism of reason, as it is set forth by Greek philosophers, appears, in comparison with the abundant light and vigour of Oriental idealism, like a feeble Promethean spark in the full flood of heavenly glory of the noonday sun—faltering and feeble, and ever ready to be extinguished.'

And with regard more especially to the Vedânta Philosophy, he says: 'The divine origin of man is continually inculcated to stimulate his efforts to return, to animate him in the struggle, and incite him to consider a reunion and reincorporation with divinity as the one primary object of every action and exertion[1].'

The Vedânta, both Philosophy and Religion.

What distinguishes the Vedânta Philosophy from all other philosophies is that it is at the same

[1] See Mana*h*sukharâma Sûryarâma, Vi*k*ârasâgara, p. 5.

time a religion and a philosophy. With us the prevailing opinion seems to be that religion and philosophy are not only different, but that they are antagonistic. It is true that there are constant attempts made to reconcile philosophy and religion. We can hardly open a Review without seeing a new Eirenicon between Science and Religion. We read not only of a Science of Religion, but even of a Religion of Science. But these very attempts, whether successful or not, show at all events that there has been a divorce between the two. And why? Philosophy as well as religion is striving after truth; then why should there be any antagonism between them? It has often been said that religion places all truth before us with authority, while philosophy appeals to the spirit of truth, that is, to our own private judgment, and leaves us perfectly free to accept or reject the doctrines of others. But such an opinion betrays a strange ignorance of the history of religions. The founder of every new religion possessed at first no greater authority than the founder of a new school of philosophy. Many of them were scorned, persecuted, and even put to death, and their last appeal was always, what it ought to be—an appeal to the spirit of truth within us, and not to twelve legions of angels, nor, as in later times, to the decrees of Councils, to Papal Bulls, or to the written letter of a sacred book. Nowhere, however, do we find what we find in India, where philosophy is looked upon as the natural outcome of religion; nay, as its most precious flower and fragrance. Whether religion leads to philosophy, or philosophy to religion, in India the two are inseparable, and they would never have been separated with us, if the fear of men had not been greater than the fear of God or of Truth. While in other countries the few who had most deeply pondered on their religion and most fully entered into the spirit of its founder, were liable to be called heretics by the ignorant many, nay were actually punished for the good work they had done in purifying religion from that crust of superstition that will always gather around it; in India the few were honoured and revered, even by those who could not yet follow them into the purer atmosphere of free and unfettered thought. Nor was there in India any necessity for honest thinkers to screen their doctrines behind the name of Esoteric Religion. If religion is to become esoteric in order to be allowed to live, as it often is with us, what is the use of it? Why should religious convictions ever fear the light of day? And, what is even more creditable to the ancient believers and philosophers of India, they never, in the exalted position which was allowed to them on account of their superior knowledge and sanctity, looked down with disdain on those who had not yet risen to their own height. They recognised the previous stages of submissive studentship and active citizenship as essential steps towards the freedom which they themselves enjoyed; nay, they admitted no one to their companionship who had not passed through these stages of passive obedience and practical usefulness. Three things they preached to them as with a voice of thunder: Damyata, Subdue yourselves, subdue the passions of the senses, of pride and selfwill; Datta, Give, be liberal and charitable to your neighbours; and Dayadhvam, Have pity on those who deserve your pity, or, as we should say, 'Love your neighbours as yourselves.' These three commands, each beginning with the syllable Da, were called the three Da's, and had to be fulfilled before any higher light was to be hoped for (B*ri*had Âra*n*yaka Upanishad V, 2), before the highest goal of the Veda, the Vedânta, could be reached.

The Upanishads as Vedânta.

Vedânta means the end of the Veda, whether we take it in the sense of the final portion, or the final object of the Veda. Now the Veda, as you know, is the old Bible of the Brâhmans, and whatever sects and systems may have sprung up within their religion during the three thousand years of its existence, they all, with the exception of course of Buddhism, agree in recognising the Veda as the highest authority on all religious questions. The Vedânta philosophy thus recognises by its very name its dependence on the Veda, and the oneness of religion and philosophy. If we take the word in its widest sense, Veda, as you know, means knowledge, but it has become the special name of the Hindu Bible, and that Bible consists of three portions, the Sa*m*hitâs, or collections of metrical prayers and hymns of praise, the Brâhma*n*as, or prose treatises on the sacrifices, and the Âra*n*yakas, books intended for the dwellers in the forest, the most important portion of which is formed by the Upanishads. These Upanishads are philosophical treatises, and their fundamental principle might seem with us to be subversive of all religion. In these Upanishads the whole ritual and sacrificial system of the Veda is not only ignored, but directly rejected as useless, nay as mischievous. The ancient gods of the Veda are no longer recognised. And yet these Upanishads are looked upon as perfectly orthodox, nay as the highest consummation of the Brahmanic religion.

This was brought about by the recognition of a very simple fact which nearly all other religions seem to have ignored. It was recognised in India from very early times that the religion of a man cannot be and ought not to be the same as that of a child; and again, that with the growth of the mind, the religious ideas of an old man must differ from those of an active man of the world. It is useless to attempt to deny such facts. We know them all from the time when we first emerge from the happy unconsciousness of a child's faith, and have to struggle with important facts that press upon us from all sides, from history, from science, and from a knowledge of the world and of ourselves. After recovering from these struggles man generally takes his stand on certain convictions which he believes that he can honestly hold and honestly defend. There are certain questions which he thinks are settled once for all and never to be opened again; there are certain arguments to which he will not even listen, because, though he has no answer to them, he does not mean to yield to them. But when the evening of life draws near and softens the lights and shades of conflicting opinions, when to agree with the spirit of truth within becomes far dearer to a man than to agree with the majority of the world without, these old questions appeal to him once more, like long-forgotten friends; he learns to bear with those from whom formerly he differed; and while he is willing to part with all that is non-essential—and most religious differences seem to arise from non-essentials—he clings all the more firmly to the few strong and solid planks that are left to carry him into the harbour, no longer very distant from his sight. It is hardly credible how completely all other religions have overlooked these simple facts, how they have tried to force on the old and wise the food that was meant for babes, and how they have thereby alienated and lost their best and strongest friends. It is therefore a lesson, all the more worth learning from history, that one religion at least, and one of the most ancient, most powerful, and most widely spread religions, has recognised this fact without the slightest hesitation.

The Four Stages of Life.

According to the ancient canons of the Brahmanic faith, each man has to pass through three or four stages. The first is that of discipline, which lasts from childhood to the age of manhood. During these years the young man is sent away from home to the house of a teacher or Guru, whom he is to obey implicitly, and to serve in every way, and who in return has to teach him all that is necessary for life, and more particularly the Veda and what pertains to his religious duties. During all that time the pupil is supposed to be a mere passive recipient, a learner and believer.

Then follows the second stage, the stage of manhood, during which a man has to marry, to rear a family, and perform all those duties which are prescribed for a householder in the Veda and the Law-books. During these two periods no doubt is ever hinted as to the truth of their religion, or the binding form of the law which everybody has to obey.

But with the third period, which begins when a man's hair has turned white, and he has seen the children of his children, a new life opens, during which the father of the family may leave his home and his village and retire into the forest with or without his wife. During that period he is absolved from the necessity of performing any sacrifices, though he may or must undergo certain self-denials and penances, some of them extremely painful. He is then allowed to meditate with perfect freedom on the great problems of life and death. And for that purpose he is expected to study the Upanishads, contained in the Âra*n*yakas or Forest-books, or rather, as books did not yet exist, he is expected to learn their doctrines from the mouth of a qualified teacher. In these Upanishads not only are all sacrificial duties rejected, but the very gods to whom the ancient prayers of the Veda were addressed, are put aside to make room for the One Supreme Being, called Bráhman[1].

Relation of the Soul (Âtman) to Brahman (the Parama-âtman).

The same Upanishads had then to explain the true relation between that Bráhman, the Supreme Being, and the soul of man. The soul of man was called Âtman, literally the self, also *G*îvâtman, the living self; and after the substantial unity of the living or individual self with the Supreme Being or Bráhman had been discovered, that Bráhman was called the Highest Self or Parama-âtman. These terms Bráhman

[1] Bráhman as a neuter is paroxytone, as a masculine oxytone, Brahmán.

and Âtman, *G*îvâtman and Paramâtman have to be carefully remembered in order to understand the Vedânta philosophy. Self, you will perceive, is a far more abstract name than soul, but it is meant to express what other nations have expressed by less abstract terms, such as *soul*, *anima*, *ψυχή* or *πνεῦμα*. Every one of these names has still something left of its original predicative power, such as moving or breathing, while âtman, self, before it was chosen as a name for soul, had become a mere pronoun, free from any metaphorical taint, and asserting nothing beyond existence or self-existence.

These terms were not new technical terms coined by philosophers. Some of them are very old terms which occur in the oldest Vedic compositions, in the hymns, the Brâhma*n*as, and finally in the Upanishads.

The etymological, that is the original, meaning of Brahman is doubtful, and it would take up too much of our time at present, were I to attempt to examine all the explanations of it which have been proposed by Indian and European scholars. I hope to return to it afterwards[1]. For the present I can only say that Brahman seems to me to have meant originally what bursts forth or breaks forth, whether in the shape of thought and word, or in the shape of creative power or physical force.

The etymology of âtman also is difficult, and this very difficulty shows that both these words, brahman and âtman, are very ancient, and, from the point of view of historical Sanskrit, belong to a prehistoric layer of Sanskrit. But whatever was the etymological meaning of âtman, whether breath or anything else, it had, in the Veda already, become a mere pronoun; it meant self, just like the Latin *ipse*, and it was *after* it meant *ipse*, that it was used to express the *ipseitas* of man, the essence or soul of man, and likewise of God.

Unsystematic Character of the Upanishads.

We can watch the growth of these thoughts in the Upanishads, and their more systematic treatment in the Vedânta-sûtras. When we read

[1] See *infra*, p. 149.

the Upanishads, the impression they leave on our mind is that they are sudden intuitions or inspirations, which sprang up here and there, and were collected afterwards. And yet there is system in all these dreams, there is a common background to all these visions. There is even an abundance of technical terms used by different speakers so exactly in the same sense, that one feels certain that behind all these lightning-flashes of religious and philosophical thought there is a distant past, a dark background of which we shall never know the beginning. There are words, there are phrases, there are whole lines and verses which recur in different Upanishads, and which must have been drawn from a common treasury; but we receive no hint as to who collected that treasury, or where it was hidden, and yet accessible to the sages of the Upanishads.

This name of Upanishad means etymologically 'sitting near a person,' the French *séance* or session, and these Upanishads may represent to us the outcome of 'sittings' or 'gatherings' which took place under the shelter of mighty trees in the forests, where old sages and their disciples met together and poured out what they had gathered during days and nights spent in quiet solitude and meditation. When we speak of forests, we must not think of a wilderness. In India the forest near the village was like a happy retreat, cool and silent, with flowers and birds, with bowers and huts. Think what their life must have been in these forests, with few cares and fewer ambitions! What should they think and talk about, if not how they came to be where they were, and what they were, and what they would be hereafter. The form of dialogue is very common in these works, and they also contain the discussions of a larger number of sages, who are so terribly earnest in their endeavours after truth that they willingly offer their heads to their adversaries, if they can prove them wrong. But while there is a complete absence of systematic teaching in these Upanishads, they offer us once more the valuable spectacle not only of what it is now the fashion to call evolution, but of real historical growth.

Growth of Religious and Philosophic Thought before the Upanishads.

There are indeed a few traces left of a previous growth in the spiritual life of the Brâhmans, and we must dwell for a moment on these antecedents of the Upanishads, in order to understand the point from whence the Vedânta philosophers started. I have often pointed out that the real importance, nay the unique character of the Veda will always be, not so much its purely chronological antiquity, great though it be, as the opportunity which it affords us of watching the active process of the fermentation of early thought. We see in the Vedic hymns the first revelation of Deity, the first expressions of surprise and suspicion, the first discovery that behind this visible and perishable world there must be something invisible, imperishable, eternal or divine. No one who has read the hymns of the Rig-veda can doubt any longer as to what was the origin of the earliest Aryan religion and mythology. Nearly all the leading deities of the Veda bear the unmistakable traces of their physical character.

Their very names tell us that they were in the beginning names of the great phenomena of nature, of fire, water, rain and storm, of sun and moon, of heaven and earth. Afterwards, we can see how these so-called deities and heroes became the centres of mythological traditions, wherever the Aryan speakers settled, whether in Asia or in Europe. This is a result gained once for all, and this light has shed its rays far beyond the Vedic mythology and religion, and lightened up the darkest corners in the history of the mythological and religious thoughts of the other Aryan nations, nay of nations unconnected by their language with the speakers of Aryan speech.

In the same way the growth of the divine idea is laid bare in the Veda as it is nowhere else. We see before our eyes who the bright powers of heaven and earth were that became the Devas, the Bright ones, or the Gods, the deities of other countries. We see how these individual and dramatic deities ceased to satisfy their early worshippers, and we find the incipient reasoners postulating One God behind all the deities of the earliest pantheon. As early a writer as Yâska about 500 B.C. has formed to himself a systematic theology, and represents all the Vedic deities as really three, those like the Fire, whose place is on earth, those like Indra, whose place is in the air, and those like the Sun, whose place is in the sky; nay he declares that it is owing to the greatness of the deity that the one Divine Self is celebrated as if it were many[1].

Belief in one God.

We see, however, in the ancient hymns already, say 1500 B.C., incipient traces of this yearning after one God. The gods, though separate individualities, are not represented as limited by other gods, but each god is for the time being implored as supreme, a phase of religious thought, which has been described by the name of Henotheism, as distinguished from the ordinary

[1] The same ideas are well summed up in one of the Upanishads (B*ri*h. Âr. Up. III, 9), where we are told that there were at first more than three thousand and three hundred gods, but that they were reduced to 33, to 6, to 3, to 2, to 1½, and at last to one, which One is the breath of life, the Self, and his name is That.

Polytheism. Thus one of the Vedic gods, Indra, the god of the air, is called Vi*s*vakarman, the Maker of all things, while the Sun (Savitar) is invoked as Pra*g*âpati, the Lord of all living beings. In some places this One as a neuter, is called the great Divinity of all the gods, mahát devắnâm asuratvám ékam (R.V. III, 55, 1).

These were indeed giant strides, and we can watch them clearly in different parts of the Veda, from the simplest invocations of the unknown agents behind sun and moon, heaven and earth, to the discovery of the One God, the Maker of heaven and earth, the Lord and Father, and lastly to the faith in one Divine Essence (Bráhman), of which the Father or Maker of all things is what they call the pratîka or face, or manifestation or, as we should say, the persona, the mask, the person.

This was the final outcome of religious thought, beginning with a most natural faith in invisible powers or agents behind the startling drama of nature, and ending with a belief in One Great Power, the unknown, or rather the unseen God, worshipped, though ignorantly worshipped, through many years by the poets of the Vedic age. It was this treasure of ancient religious thought which the sages of the Upanishads inherited from their forefathers, and we shall now have to see what use they made of it, and how they discovered at last the true relation between what we call the Divine or the Infinite, as seen objectively in nature, and the Divine or the Infinite as perceived subjectively in the soul of man. We shall then be better able to understand how they erected on this ancient foundation what was at the same time the most sublime philosophy and the most satisfying religion, the Vedânta.

Two Forms of the Vedânta.

When we speak of Vedânta philosophy we must distinguish between two forms in which we possess it. We possess it in an unsystematic form, nay as a kind of wild growth in the Upanishads, and we have it once more, carefully elaborated, and fully systematized in the Vedânta-sûtras. These Sûtras are ascribed to Bâdarâya*n*a [1],

---

[1] This Vyâsa Bâdarâya*n*a can hardly be, as Weber and others

whose date, as usual, is disputed. They do not form a book, in our sense of the word, for they are really no more than headings containing the quintessence of the Vedânta philosophy. By themselves they would be completely unintelligible, but if learnt by heart, as they were and still are, they would no doubt form a very useful thread through the labyrinth of the Vedânta. By the side of these Sûtras, however, there must always have existed a body of oral teaching, and it was probably this traditional teaching which was gathered up at last by *S*ankara, the famous teacher of the Vedânta, in his so-called commentary or Bhâshya on the Sûtras. That Bhâshya, however, so far from being a mere commentary, may in fact be regarded as the real body of the Vedânta doctrines, to which the Sûtras form no more than a useful index. Yet these Sûtras must soon have acquired an independent authority, for

supposed, the same as the Vyâsa Dvaipâyana, the reputed author of the Mahâbhârata. The character of their works is different, and so are their names. Bâdarâya*n*a, the author of the Brahma-sûtras, is generally referred to about 400 A.D., though without very conclusive evidence.

they were interpreted in different ways by different philosophers, by *S*añkara, by Râmânu*g*a[1], Madhva, Vallabha, and others, who became the founders of different Vedânta[2] sects, all appealing to the Sûtras as their highest authority.

The most extraordinary feature of this Vedânta philosophy consists, as I remarked before, in its being an independent system of philosophy, yet

[1] We are told in the Sarvadar*s*ana-sañgraha (p. 80, transl. Cowell) that Râmânu*g*a, who lived in the twelfth century, found the previous commentary composed by Bodhâyana too prolix, and therefore composed his own. Râmânu*g*a says so himself in his *S*rîbhâshya, and informs us that other teachers before him had done the same (Ved.-sûtras, transl. Thibaut, vol. i, p. xxi). If the V*ri*ttikâra against whom some of *S*añkara's remarks are said to be intended is the same Bodhâyana, his date would be previous at least to 700 A.D.

[2] In some cases the different expositors of the Vedânta-sûtras do actual violence to the text. Thus in I, 1, 15 the text of the Sûtras is Vikâra-*s*abdân na iti *k*en na prâ*k*uryât. This is meant to show that the suffix maya in ânandamaya does not necessarily convey the idea of change or degree, which would not be applicable to Brahman, but that it conveys the idea of abundance (prâ*k*urya). But Vallabha explains prâ*k*uryât not as an ablative but as a compound prâ*k*urya-at, i.e. going towards or reaching abundance, because this material world itself is Brahman, which has attained to the condition of abundance. (Sha*d*dar*s*ana-*k*intanikâ III, p. 39.)

entirely dependent on the Upanishads, a part of the Veda, nay chiefly occupied with proving that all its doctrines, to the very minutest points, are derived from the revealed doctrines of the Upanishads, if only properly understood, that they are in perfect harmony with revelation, and that there are no contradictions whatever between the various Upanishads themselves.

Upanishads treated as Revealed, not as Historical Books.

It was necessary to do this, for the Upanishads were believed to be divine revelation, and this belief was so firmly established that even the boldest philosophers in India had to reconcile their own doctrines with those of their ancient inspired teachers. This is done with the most extraordinary ingenuity and a perseverance worthy of a better cause[1]. To us the Upanishads have,

[1] Thus in the commentary on Ved.-sûtras II, 1, 11, we read: 'In matters to be known from Scripture mere reasoning is not to be relied on for the following reason also. As the thoughts of men are altogether unfettered, reasoning which disregards

of course, a totally different interest. We watch in them the historical growth of philosophical

the holy texts, and rests on individual opinion only, has no proper foundation. We see how arguments, which some clever men had excogitated with great pains, are shown, by people still more ingenious, to be fallacious, and how the arguments of the latter again are refuted in their turn by other men; so that, on account of the diversity of men's opinions, it is impossible to accept mere reasoning as having a sure foundation. Nor can we get over this difficulty by accepting as well-founded the reasoning of some person of recognised mental eminence, may he be Kapila or anybody else; since we observe that even men of the most undoubted mental eminence, such as Kapila, Ka*n*âda, and other founders of philosophical schools, have contradicted one another.' It is true that this line of reasoning is objected to because in reasoning against reasoning, we implicitly admit the authority of reason. But in the end *S*añkara holds that 'the true nature of the cause of the world, on which final emancipation depends, cannot, on account of its excessive abstruseness, even be thought of without the help of the holy texts.' 'The Veda,' he adds, 'which is eternal and the source of knowledge, may be allowed to have for its object firmly established things, and hence the perfection of that knowledge which is founded on the Veda cannot be denied by any of the logicians of the past, present, or future. We have thus established the perfection of this our knowledge which reposes on the Upanishads.'

See also II, 1, 27: 'As the Purâ*n*a says: "Do not apply reasoning to what is unthinkable! The mark of the unthinkable is that it is above all material causes." Therefore the cognition of what is supersensuous is based on the holy texts thought, and are not offended therefore by the variety of their opinions. On the contrary, we expect to find variety, and are even pleased when we find independent thought and apparent contradictions between individual teachers, although the general tendency of all is the same. Thus we find side by side such utterances as 'In the beginning there was Bráhman,' 'In the beginning there was Self,' 'In the beginning there was water,' 'In the beginning there was nothing,' 'In the beginning there was something,' or to translate these two sentences more correctly into the language of our European philosophy, 'In the beginning there was the μὴ ὄν,' and 'In the

only. But—our opponent will say—even the holy texts cannot make us understand what is contradictory. Bráhman, you say, which is without parts undergoes a change, but not the entire Bráhman. If Bráhman is without parts, it does either not change at all, or it changes in its entirety. If, on the other hand, it is said that it changes partly and persists partly, a break is effected in its nature, and from that it follows that it consists of parts, &c.' Here *S*añkara admits a real difficulty, but he explains it away by showing that the break in Bráhman is the result of Avidyâ (nescience) only. The same reasoning is applied in II, 1, 31 and elsewhere.

beginning there was τὸ ὄν.' We meet even in the Upanishads themselves with discussions provoked by these contradictory statements and intended to reconcile them, as when we read in the *Kh*ând. Up. VI, 27, 'But how could that which is, be born of that which is not? No, my son, that only which is, was in the beginning, one only, without a second[1].' But while in the Upanishads these various guesses at truth seem thrown out at haphazard, they were afterwards woven together with wonderful patience and ingenuity.[2] The uniform purpose running through all of them, was clearly brought out, and a system of philosophy was erected out of such diverse materials, which is not only perfectly coherent, but quite clear and distinct on almost every point of doctrine. Though here and there the Sûtras admit of divergent interpretations, no doubt is left on any important point of *S*añkara's philosophy; which is more than can be said of any system of philosophy from the days of Plato to the days of Kant.

[1] See Taitt. Up. II, 7, Sacred Books of the East, xv, p. 58.

[2] See Vedânta-sûtras I, 4, 14–15.

Moral Preparation for the Study of the Vedânta.

The study of philosophy in India was not only an integral part of the religion of the Brâhmans, but it was based from the very beginning on a moral foundation. We saw already that no one was admitted to the study of the Upanishads who had not been properly initiated and introduced by a qualified teacher, and who had not fulfilled the duties, both civil and religious, incumbent on a householder. But even that was not enough. No one was supposed to be fit for true philosophical speculation who had not completely subdued his passions. The sea must no longer be swept by storms, if it is to reflect the light of the sun in all its divine calmness and purity. Hence, even the hermit in the forest was expected to be an ascetic, and to endure severe penances as a help for extinguishing all the passions that might disturb his peace. And it was not only the body that had to be subdued and hardened against all external disturbances such as heat and cold, hunger and thirst. Six things had to be acquired by the mind, namely tranquillity[1], restraint, self-denial, long-suffering, collectedness, and faith. It has been thought[2] that this quietness is hardly the best outfit for a philosopher, who, according to our views of philosophy, is to pile Ossa on Pelion in order to storm the fortress of truth and to conquer new realms in earth and heaven. But we must remember that the object of the Vedânta was to show that we have really nothing to conquer but ourselves, that we possess everything within us, and that nothing is required but to shut our eyes and our hearts against the illusion of the world in order to find ourselves richer than heaven and earth. Even faith, *s*raddhâ[3], which has given special offence as a requisite for philosophy, because philosophy, according to Descartes, ought to begin with *de omnibus dubitare*, has its legitimate place in the Vedânta philosophy, for, like Kant's philosophy, it leads us on to see that many things are beyond

[1] *S*ama, Dama, Uparati (often explained as relinquishment of all sacrificial duties), Titikshâ, Samâdhi, *S*raddhâ.

[2] Deussen, System, p. 85.

[3] It is left out in some texts.

the limits of human understanding, and must be accepted or believed, without being understood.

How seriously and religiously philosophy was taken up by the Vedântists, we see from what are considered the essential requisites of a true philosopher. He ought to have surrendered all desire for rewards in this life or in the life to come. He ought therefore never to dream of acquiring wealth, of founding a school, of gaining a name in history; he ought not even to think of any recompense in a better life. All this may sound very unreal, but I cannot help thinking that in ancient India these things were real, for why should they have been imagined? Life was as yet so simple, so unartificial, that there was no excuse for unrealities. The ancient Brahmans never seem to pose—they hardly had a public to pose to. There were no other nations to watch them, or if there were, they were barbarians in the eyes of the Brahmans, and their applause would have counted for nothing. I do not mean to say that the ancient Hindu philosophers were made altogether of a better stuff than we ourselves. I only mean that many of the temptations to which our modern philosophers succumb, did not exist in the days of the Upanishads. Without wishing to draw any disparaging comparisons, I thought it necessary to point out some of the advantages which the ancient thinkers of India enjoyed in their solitude, in order to account for the extraordinary fact that after 2,000 years their works are still able to rivet our attention, while with us, in spite of advertisements, of friendly and unfriendly reviews, the philosophical book of the season is so often the book of one season only. In India the prevailing philosophy is still the Vedânta, and now that printing of ancient Sanskrit texts has set in and become profitable, there are more new editions published of the Upanishads and *S*ankara in India[1], than of Descartes and Spinoza in Europe. Why is that? I believe much of the excellency of the ancient Sanskrit philosophers is due to their having been undisturbed by the thought of there being a public to please or critics to appease. They thought of nothing but the

[1] See Catalogues of Sanskrit Books in the British Museum, by Haas and Bendall, s.v. Bâdarâya*n*a.

work they had determined to do: their one idea was to make it as perfect as it could be made. There was no applause they valued, unless it came from their equals or their betters; publishers, editors, and log-rollers did not yet exist. Need we wonder then that their work was done as well as it could be done, and that it has lasted for thousands of years? The ancient Upanishads describe the properly qualified student of philosophy in the following words (B*ri*h. Up. IV, 4, 23): 'He therefore who knows the Self, after having become quiet, subdued, satisfied, patient, and collected, sees self in Self, sees all as Self. Evil does not overcome him, he overcomes all evil. Evil does not burn him, he burns all evil. Free from evil, free from spots, free from doubt, he becomes a true Brâhma*n*a.'

Mistrust in the Evidence of the Senses.

Another essential requisite for a student of philosophy was the power to distinguish between what is eternal and what is not. This distinction lies no doubt at the root of all philosophy.

Philosophy begins when men, after having gazed on the world, suddenly stare and start, and ask, What art thou? There are minds perfectly satisfied with things as they appear, and quite incapable of apprehending anything except what is visible and tangible. They would hardly know what is meant by anything invisible or eternal, least of all could they bring themselves to believe that what is invisible is alone real and eternal, while what is visible is by its very nature unreal or phenomenal only, changeable, perishable, and non-eternal. And yet they might have learnt from St. Paul (2 Cor. iv. 18) that the things which are seen are temporal; but the things which are not seen, eternal. To the Brâhmans to be able to mistrust the evidence of the senses was the very first step in philosophy, and they had learnt from the remotest times the lesson that all secondary, nay all primary qualities also, are and can be subjective only. In later times they reduced these ancient philosophical intuitions to a system, and they reasoned them out with an exactness which may well excite our surprise and admiration.

Metaphorical Language of the Upanishads.

In the earliest period of philosophic thought, however, which is represented to us by some of the Upanishads, they were satisfied with prophetic visions, and these were often expressed in pregnant metaphors only. The phenomenal world was to them like the mirage of the desert, visible, but unreal, exciting thirst, but never quenching it. The terror of the world was like the fright occasioned by what seemed a snake in the dark, but in the light of day or of truth, proved to be a rope only. If asked why the Infinite should be perceived by us as qualified, they answered: Look at the air in the sky, it is not blue; yet we cannot help seeing it as blue. If asked how the One Infinite Being, the One without a Second, could appear as many in this world, they said: Look at the waves of the sea, and the ripples in the rivers and the lakes: in every one there is the sun reflected a thousand-fold—yet we know that there is but one sun, though our eyes cannot bear its great glory and its dazzling light.

It is interesting, however, to observe how carefully *S*aṅkara guards against the abuse of metaphorical illustration. He knows that *omne simile claudicat.* An illustrative simile, he says very truly, is meant to illustrate *one* point only, not all; otherwise it would not be a simile. He goes on to remark that the comparison of Bráhman or the Highest Self, as reflected in the variety of this universe, with the sun or moon, as reflected in the water, may seem not quite admissible, because the sun has a certain form, and comes in contact with the water which is different from it and at a distance from it. Here we can understand that there should be an image of the sun in the water. But the Âtman or the Highest Self has no form, and as it is present everywhere and all is identical with it, there are no limiting conditions different from it. But he continues, if therefore it should be objected that the two instances are not parallel, we answer: 'The parallel instance (of the sun's reflection in the water) holds good, since *one* common feature—with reference to which alone the comparison is instituted—does exist. Whenever two things are compared, they are so with reference to some particular point only which they are thought to have in common. Entire equality between two things can never be demonstrated; indeed if it could be demonstrated, there would be an end of that particular relation which gives rise to a comparison.' *S*añkara therefore was fully aware of the dangerous nature of comparisons which have often done so much mischief in philosophical and religious discussions, by being extended beyond their proper limits. But even then he is not yet satisfied. He seems to say, I am not answerable for the comparison; it occurs in the Veda itself, and whatever occurs in the Veda, must be right. This shows that even a belief in literal inspiration is not a new invention. He then adds that the special feature on which the comparison rests is only the participation 'in the increase and decrease.' What he means is that the reflected image of the sun expands, when the surface of the water expands, and contracts when the water contracts; that it trembles when the water trembles, and divides when the water is divided. It thus participates in all the attributes and conditions of the water; while the real sun remains all the time the same. Similarly the Bráhman, the Supreme Being, although in reality uniform and never changing, participates, as it were, in the attributes and states of the body and the other limiting conditions (or upâdhis) within which it abides; it grows with them as it were, decreases with them as it were, and so on. Hence, as two things compared possess certain features in common, no valid objection can be made to the comparison.

This will show you that, however poetical and sometimes chaotic the language of the Upanishads may be, *S*aṅkara, the author of the great commentary on the Vedânta-sûtras, knows how to reason accurately and logically, and would be able to hold his own against any opponent, whether Indian or European.

There is another well-known simile in the Upanishads, intended to illustrate the doctrine that Brahman is both the material and the efficient cause of the world, that the world is made not only by God, but also of God. How can that be? the pupil asks, and his teacher answers: 'Look at the spider who with the utmost intelligence draws the threads of its wonderful net out of its own body.' What he meant was of course no more than an illustration that should help his pupil to understand what was meant by Bráhman being at the same time the material and the efficient cause of the web of the created world. But what has been the consequence? Some of the earliest missionaries related that the god of the Brahmans was a large black spider sitting in the centre of the universe, and creating the world by drawing it out like threads from its own body.

Comparisons, you see, are dangerous things, unless they are used cautiously, and though the Upanishads abound with poetical metaphors we shall see that no one could have availed himself of these philosophical similes with greater caution than *S*ankara, the author of the classical work on the Vedânta philosophy.

LECTURE II.

THE SOUL AND GOD.

Extracts from the Upanishads. I. From the Ka*th*a Upanishad.

I SHALL to-day give you first of all a few specimens of the style in which the Upanishads are written.

In one of the Upanishads we read of a father who glories in having made a complete and perfect sacrifice by surrendering all that he could call his own, to the gods. Thereupon his son, his only son, seems to have taunted him with not having sacrificed him also to the gods. This has been considered as a survival of human sacrifices in India, just as Abraham's willingness to sacrifice Isaac has been accepted as a proof of the former existence of similar sacrifices among the Hebrews. It may be so, but nothing is said in our case of a real killing of the son. After the father has said that he would give his son to Death, we find at once that the son has entered the abode of Death (Yama Vaivasvata), and that, in the absence of Death, there is no one to receive him with the honours due to a Brâhman. Hence when the lord of the Departed, Yama, returns after three days' absence, he expresses his regret, and offers the young man three boons to choose. The young philosopher asks first that his father may not be angry with him, when he returns (so he evidently means to return to life), and secondly that he may acquire the knowledge of certain sacrificial acts which lead to happiness in Paradise. But for the third boon he will accept nothing but a knowledge of what becomes of man after death. 'There is that doubt,' he says, 'when a man is dead, some saying, he is; others, he is not. This I should like to know, taught by thee, this is the third of my boons.'

Yama, the god of death, declines to answer that question, and tempts the young man with every kind of gift, promising him wealth, beautiful women, a long life, and pleasures of every kind. But his guest resists and says (I, 26): 'These things last till to-morrow, O Death, and they wear out the vigour of our senses. Even the whole of our life is short. Keep thy horses, keep dance and song for thyself. No man can be made happy by wealth. Shall we possess wealth, when we see thee, O Death?'

In the end Death has to yield. He has promised the three boons, and he must fulfil his promise. All this throws a bright light on the state of life and the state of thought in India, say 3,000 years ago. For although all this is poetry, we must remember that poetry always presupposes reality, and that no poets could have successfully appealed to human sympathy, unless they had struck chords which could vibrate in response.

Then Yama says: 'After pondering on all pleasures that are or seem delightful, thou hast dismissed them all. Thou hast not gone into the road that leadeth to wealth, by which many go to destruction. Fools dwelling in darkness, wise in their own conceit, and puffed up with vain knowledge, go round and round, staggering to and fro, like blind men led by the blind. The Hereafter never rises before the eyes of the thoughtless child, deluded by the delusion of wealth. "This is the world," he thinks, "there is no other"—and thus he falls again and again under my sway'—the sway of death.

After Yama has convinced himself that his young Brâhman guest has subdued all passions, and that neither sacrifice nor faith in the ordinary gods, nor hope for happiness in heaven, will satisfy him, he begins to indicate to him the true nature of the Bráhman, which forms the eternal reality of the world, in order to lead him on to see the oneness of his soul, that is, of his self with Bráhman; for this, according to the Upanishads, is true immortality. 'The Self,' he says, 'smaller than small, greater than great, is hidden in the heart of the creature. A man who is free from desires and free from grief, sees the majesty of the Self by the grace of the Creator[1].'

---

[1] It is very tempting to read dhâtuprasâdât, and to translate 'from the quieting of the elements,' taking elements in the sense of the three Gu*n*as, sattvam, ra*g*as, and tamas; see *G*âbâla Up. IV. But the same expression dhâtu*h* prasâdât occurs again in the *S*vetâ*s*vatara Upanishad III, 20 and in the Mahânârây. Up. VIII, 3; while the compound dhâtuprasâda does not occur in the Upanishads, nor is prasâda ever used of the equalisation of the gu*n*as, but constantly of the favour or grace of personal beings (Î*s*vara, &c.).

'That Self cannot be gained by the Veda nor by understanding, nor by much learning. He whom the Self chooses, by him the Self can be gained. The Self chooses him as his own.'

This idea that the knowledge of Self does not come by study nor by good works, but by the grace or the free choice of the Self, is familiar to the authors of the Upanishads, but it is not the same as what was called before the grace of the Creator.

Then he goes on: 'No mortal lives by the breath that goes up and by the breath that goes down,—what we should call the breath of life. We live by another, in whom these two repose.'—Here we see that the Brâhmans had clearly perceived the difference between the organic life of the body, and the existence of the Self, a difference which many philosophers of much later times have failed to perceive.

And again: 'He, the highest Person, who is awake in men[1] while they are asleep, shaping one lovely sight after another, that indeed is the

[1] It would introduce a thoroughly modern idea to translate 'The spirit who watches over those who sleep.' Nor does atyeti mean 'to escape.'

Bright, that is Bráhman, that alone is called the Immortal. All worlds are contained in it, and no one goes beyond.'

'As the one fire, after it has entered the world, though one, becomes like unto every form which it takes (like unto whatever it burns), thus the one Self within all things becomes different, according to whatever it enters,—but it exists also without.'

'As the sun, the eye of the whole world, is not contaminated by the external impurities seen by the eyes, thus the one Self within all things is never contaminated by the misery of the world, being himself without.'

Here you see the transcendent character of the Self maintained, even after it has become incarnate, just as we hold that God is present in all things, but also transcends them (Westcott, St. John, p. 160). Again, he says: 'There is one ruler, the Self within all things, who makes the one form manifold. The wise who perceive him within their self or soul, to them belongs eternal happiness, not to others.'

'His form is not to be seen, no one beholds him with the eye. He is imaged by the heart, by wisdom, by the mind. Those who know this are immortal.'

It is remarkable how little the mind of the author of this Upanishad, whoever he may have been, is concerned with anything like proving the immortality of the soul by arguments. And the same applies to the religions of most of the ancient people of the world, nay, even to the religions of savage and uncivilized races with whose opinions concerning the soul and its fate after death we are acquainted. No attempt is ever made to collect arguments in support of the soul's immortality, for the simple reason, it would seem, that though there was undeniable evidence of the decay and final decomposition of the body, nothing like the death of the soul had ever come within human cognizance. The ideas as to the manner of life which the soul would lead after death are, no doubt, often very childish and imperfect, but the idea that the soul would come to a complete end after the death of the body, the most childish and imperfect of all ideas, belongs decidedly to a later age. Like other sacred writings, the Upanishads also indulged in the most fanciful descriptions of the abode of the soul after death, and their conceptions of the happiness or unhappiness of the departed spirits are hardly superior to those of the Greeks. It may have been the very fancifulness of these descriptions that raised the doubts of more serious thinkers, and thus made them throw up their belief in the vulgar immortality of the souls, together with their old belief in Elysian fields and Isles of the Blessed. The Upanishads, however, adopt a much wiser course. They do not argue against the popular belief, they leave the old belief as useful to those who know no higher happiness than an increase of the happiness which they enjoyed in this life, and who, by good works, had deserved the fulfilment of their human hopes and wishes. But they reserve a higher immortality, or rather the only true immortality, for those who had gained a knowledge of the eternal Bráhman and of their identity with it, and who could as little doubt of their existence after death, as they doubted of their existence before death. They knew that their true being, like that of Bráhman, was without beginning and therefore without end, and they were wise enough not to indulge in any prophetic visions as to the exact form which their future existence would assume. Immortality is represented as the result of knowledge. Man is immortal as soon as he knows himself, or rather his self, that is, as soon as he knows the eternal Self within him.

The whole of this philosophy may be called the common property of the ancient thinkers of India. It was natural enough that it should not have been taught to children or to people unfit as yet for higher thought; but no person qualified by birth and education was kept from it. All that strikes us is a certain reticence, even on the part of Death, when he is made to communicate his knowledge to his young guest. We see that the teacher is fully aware of the high value of his knowledge, and that he entrusts it to his pupil rather grudgingly, and as the most precious thing he has to give.

II. From the Maitrâya*n*a Upanishad.

We shall see the same hesitation in another episode taken from the Maitrâya*n*a Upanishad.

Here it is not a young Brâhman, but an old king who had surrendered the crown to his son and retired into the forest to meditate on life and death. He there meets a wise hermit, and throws himself at his feet, saying: 'O Saint, I know not the Self, thou knowest its essence. Teach it to me.'

Here also the teacher tells the king at first that what he asks is difficult to teach. But the king insists. 'What is the use of the enjoyment of pleasures,' he says, 'in this offensive, unsubstantial body—a mere mass of bones, skin, sinews, marrow, flesh, seed, blood, mucus, tears, phlegm, ordure, water, bile and slime? What is the need of the enjoyment of pleasures in this body which is assailed by lust, hatred, greed, delusion, fear, anguish, jealousy, separation from what we love, union with what we do not love, hunger, thirst, old age, death, illness, grief and other evils? We see that all is perishable, like these insects, like herbs and trees, growing and decaying. Mighty rulers of empires, wielders of bows—then follows a long list of names—have before the eyes of their whole family surrendered the greatest happiness and passed on from this world to the next. Great oceans have been dried up, mountains have fallen, even the pole-star moves[1], the ropes that hold the stars have been cut[2], the earth has been submerged[3] and the very gods have fled from their places. In such a world as this, what is the use of the enjoyment of pleasures, if he who has fed on them has to return again and again!'—(You see here the fear of another life; the fear, not of death, but of birth, which runs through the whole of Indian philosophy.) 'Deign therefore,' he says, 'to take me out. In this world I am like a frog in a dry well. O Saint, thou art the way, thou art my way.'

Then follows the teaching, not, however, from the teacher's own mind, but as he himself had been taught by another teacher, called Maitri. And Maitri, again, is not represented as what we should call the author, but he also relates only what had been revealed by Pragâpati, the lord of

[1] Probably the earliest references to the procession of the equinoxes.

[2] This may refer to shooting stars or to comets.

[3] This may refer to the tradition of a deluge.

creatures, to some other saints, the Vâlakhilyas. All this shows a distant historical background, and however fanciful some of the details may seem to us, we get the impression that the life described in these Upanishads was a real life, that in the very remotest times the settlers in that beautiful and over-fertile country were occupied in reasoning out the thoughts which are recorded in the Upanishads, that they were really a race of men different from us, different from any other race, that they cared more for invisible than for visible things, and that kings and princes among them really descended from their thrones and left their palaces, in order to meditate in the dark and cool groves of their forests, on the unsolved problems of life and death. At a much later time Gautama Buddha did the same, and it would be carrying historical scepticism too far were we to doubt his having been the son of a prince or nobleman who gave up his throne and everything he possessed, in order to become a philosopher and afterwards a teacher. When we see how his success among the people depended on the very fact of his having sacrificed crown and wealth, wife and child, to become a Buddha and a saviour; nay, when we see how one of the strongest reproaches addressed to him by the Brâhmans was that he, being a Kshatriya or nobleman, should have ventured to assume the office of a spiritual teacher, we can hardly doubt that we are dealing here with historical facts, however they may have been embellished by his enthusiastic followers.

In our Upanishad the first question asked is: 'O Saint, this body is without intelligence, like a cart. By whom has this body been made intelligent, and who is the driver of it?' Then Pra*g*âpati answers that it is He who is standing above, passionless amidst the objects of the world, endless, imperishable, unborn and independent, that it is Bráhman that made this body intelligent and is the driver of it.

Then a new question follows, namely, How a being without passions and desires could have been moved to do this, and the answer is somewhat mythological, for we are told that Pra*g*âpati (Vi*s*va) stood alone in the beginning, that he had no happiness when alone, and that meditating on himself he created many creatures. He looked on them and saw they were like stone, without understanding, and standing about like lifeless posts. He had no happiness, and thought he would enter into them that they might awake. This he achieved in his own peculiar way, and then became the subjective principle within them, though he himself remained unmoved and undefiled. Then follow physiological and psychological details, which we may pass over. There follow beautiful passages declaring the presence of Brahman in the sun and in other parts of nature; but the end is always the same, that 'He who is in the fire, and He who is in the heart, and He who is in the sun, are all one and the same,' and that he who knows this becomes one with the One (VI, 17). 'As birds and deer do not approach a burning mountain, so sins never approach those who know Bráhman.' And again (VI, 20), 'Through the serenity of this thought he kills all actions, good or bad; his self serene, abiding in the Self, obtains imperishable bliss.'

'Thoughts alone,' he says, 'cause the round

of a new birth and a new death; let a man therefore strive to purify his thoughts. What a man thinks, that he is: this is the old secret[1] (VI, 34). If the thoughts of men were so fixed on the Eternal or Bráhman, as they are on the things of this world, who would not be freed from bondage?' When a man, having freed his mind from sloth, distraction, and unrest, becomes as it were delivered from his mind, that is the highest point. 'Water in water, fire in fire, ether in ether, no one can distinguish them; likewise a man whose mind has entered into the Eternal, into Bráhman, obtains liberty.'

Sankara's Analysis of Subject and Object.

We shall now have to see how wonderful a system of philosophy has been built up with such materials by the author or authors of the Vedânta Philosophy. Here the scattered fragments are carefully arranged and systematically

[1] Exactly the same idea is expressed by Buddha in the first verse of the Dhammapada (Sacred Books of the East, x, p. 3): 'All that we are is the result of what we have thought: it is founded on our thoughts, it is made up of our thoughts.'

put together, one step follows after another, and the thread of the argument is never broken or lost. The so-called Vedânta-sûtras cannot be translated, and if translated they would convey as little sense as the different headings in the programme of my lectures. I shall try, however, to give you a specimen of the style of *S*ankara, to whom we owe the elaborate commentary on these Sûtras, and who is indeed the principal representative of the Vedânta philosophy in the literary history of India. But I must warn you that his style, though much more like the style of an ordinary book, is difficult to follow, and requires the same effort of attention which we have to bestow on the intricate arguments of Aristotle or Kant.

'As it is well known,' *S*añkara says, in the very beginning of his work, 'that object and subject, which fall under the perception of *We* and *You* (or, as we should say, of the Ego and Non-Ego), are in their very essence opposed to each other like darkness and light, and that therefore one cannot take the place of the other, it follows all the more that their attributes also cannot be interchanged.' What he means is that subject and object, or what falls under the names of *We* and *You*, are not only different from each other, but diametrically opposed and mutually exclusive, so that what is conceived as the object can never be conceived as the subject of a sentence, and *vice versâ*. We can never think or say 'We are You,' or 'You are We,' nor ought we ever to substitute subjective for objective qualities. Thus, for instance, the *You* may be seen and heard and touched, but the *We* or the *I* can never be seen, heard, or touched. Its being is its knowing, not its being known.

Having established this general proposition, *S*aṅkara continues: 'Therefore we may conclude that to transfer what is objective, that is what is perceived as *You*, the Non-Ego and its qualities, on what is subjective, that is what is perceived as *We*, the Ego, which consists of thought, or *vice versâ* to transfer what is subjective on what is objective, must be altogether wrong. A subject can never be anything but a subject, the object always remains the object.

'Nevertheless,' he continues, 'it is a habit

inherent in human nature, a necessity of thought, we should call it, something which human nature cannot shake off, to say, combining what is true and what is false, "I am this, and this is mine." This is a habit caused by a false apprehension of subjects and predicates which are absolutely different, and by not distinguishing one from the other, but transferring the essence and the qualities of the one upon the other.'

You can easily see that subject and object are not used by *S*añkara in their merely logical sense, but that by subject he means what is true and real, in fact the Self, whether divine or human, while objective means with him what is phenomenal and unreal, such as the body with its organs, and the whole visible world. Combining the two, such statements as 'I am strong or I am weak, I am blind or I can see,' form the false apprehension which, he admits, is inherent in human nature, but which nevertheless is wrong, and has to be weakened, and finally to be destroyed by the Vedânta philosophy.

Then follows a disquisition as to what is meant by this act of transference whereby what is the subject is made objective. All definitions seem to agree in this that this transference consists in imagining in one's mind or memory that one recognises something seen before, but that one sees it somewhere else. As an illustration he gives the fact that some people mistake mother-of-pearl for silver, that is, transfer the essence and qualities seen in silver on mother-of-pearl. Or again, that some people imagine they see two moons, though they know perfectly well that there is only one. In the same manner people imagine that the living being or the ordinary Ego is the true subject or self, or that there are two real selves, the body and the soul, though there can be only one, which is all in all. The nature of this transference which lies at the root of all mundane experience or illusion, is once more explained as 'taking a thing for what it is not,' which is illustrated by a compassionate man saying it fares badly with him and that he is miserable, though he himself is quite well, and it is his wife and children only who are suffering. In a similar way a man says that he is fat, or thin, that he moves, stands, or springs, that he does anything, that he wishes for this or for that, while in truth, he himself, that is, his true self, the ideal subject, is only the witness of all this doing and wishing, the looker on, who is or ought to be quite independent of the various states of the body.

In conclusion *S*aṅkara sums up by saying that all that is founded on this wrong transference or assumption, all in fact that we know and believe to be true, whether in science, or ordinary philosophy, or law, or anything else, belongs to the realm of Avidyâ or Nescience, and that it is the aim of the Vedânta Philosophy to dispel that Nescience, and to replace it by Vidyâ, or true knowledge.

This kind of reasoning may sound strange to us who are accustomed to quite a different atmosphere of thought, but it contains nevertheless an important thought, and one that has never, so far as I know, been fully utilized by European philosophers, namely, the fundamental incompatibility between what is subjective and what is objective; nay, the impossibility of the subject ever becoming an object, or an object the subject.

Subject, with the Vedântists, is not a logical but a metaphysical term. It is, in fact, another name for self, soul, spirit or whatever name has been given to the eternal element in man and God. European philosophers, whatever they may hold about the soul, always speak of it as something that can be known and described, and therefore may form a possible object. If the Hindu philosopher is clear on any point it is this, that the subjective soul, the witness or knower, or the Self, can never be known as objective, but can only be itself, and thus be conscious of itself.

*S*ankara would never allow that the self or the subject could be known as an object. We can only know ourselves by being ourselves; and if other people think they know us, they know our phenomenal self, our Ego only, never our subjective self, because that can never be anything but a subject; it knows, but it cannot be known. The same, if we imagine that we know others, what we know is what is visible, knowable, that is the appearance, but never the all-pervading self. So again if we transfer to what is objective only, such as the sky, or a river, or a mountain, a subjective selfhood, we go wrong, we produce mythology and idolatry—we gain false, not true knowledge.

When we say that the whole world is divided into a visible and an invisible world, into phenomena and noümena, the Vedântist would say that there is a subjective and an objective world, and that what is subjective in their sense of the word can never be perceived as objective nor *vice versâ.* Psychologists may imagine that they can treat, the soul as an object of knowledge, dissect it and describe it. The Vedântist would say, that what they dissect and weigh and analyse and describe is not the soul, in his sense of the word, it is not the subject, it is not the self in the highest sense of the word. What they call perception, memory, conception, what they call will and effort, all this, according to the Vedântist, is outside the self, and even in its most perfect and sublime manifestations is nothing but the veil through which the eternal self looks at the world. Of the self behind the veil, we can know nothing beyond that it is, and this too we know in a way different from all other knowledge. We know it by being it, just as the sun may be said to shine by its own light, and by that light to lighten the whole world.

The nearest approach to what *S*aṅkara means by subject and object is found, I believe, in Schopenhauer's *Wille* and *Vorstellung*, his *Will* corresponding to Bráhman, or the subject of the world, the only true reality, his *Vorstellung* to the phenomenal world, as seen by us objectively, and to be recognised as unreal, changeable and perishable. These ideas are perfectly familiar to the authors of the Upanishads. With them therefore true immortality consists simply and entirely in the self knowing his self. Thus in a famous dialogue [1] between Yâ*g*ñavalkya and his wife Maitrêyî, who wishes to follow her husband into the forest and to learn from him what the soul is, and what is immortality, Yâ*g*ñavalkya sums up all he has to say in the following words: 'Verily, beloved one, the Self, i.e. the soul, is imperishable and of an indestructible nature. For, when there is, as it were, duality, then one

[1] B*ri*h. Âr. Upanishad IV, 6; S. B. E. xv, p. 185.

sees the other, one hears the other, one perceives the other, one knows the other. But when the Self only is all this, how should he see another, how should he hear another, how should he perceive or know another? How should he know Him, by whom he knows all? That Self can only be described by "No, no" (that is by protesting against every attribute). That Self is incomprehensible, he is imperishable, he is unattached, he is unfettered. How, O beloved one, should he, the knower, know the knower?'

Here is the critical point. How should the knower know the knower? or, as we should say, How can the soul know the soul? He can only be the knower, he in whom subject and object are one, or rather, in whom there is no distinction between subject and object, between knowing and being known, whose very being is knowing and whose knowing is being. As soon as the Self is conceived and changed into something objective, Nescience steps in, the illusory cosmic life begins, the soul seems to be this or that, to live and to die, while as a subject, it can be touched by neither life nor death—it stands aloof, it is immortal. 'That is true immortality,' as Yâ*gñ*a-valkya said, and with these words he went away into the forest.

The Inheritance of the Vedânta.

Let us now look back on what I called the ancient inheritance of the Vedânta philosophers. We saw that they had inherited a concept, slowly elaborated in the Vedic hymns and Brâhma*n*as, that of Bráhman, that is, that from which, as the Vedânta-sûtras say, the origin, subsistence and dissolution of this world proceed (Vedânta-sûtras I, 2). The only attributes of this Bráhman, if attributes they can be called, are that he is, that he knows, and that he is full of bliss.

But if that is the highest concept of the Supreme Being, of Bráhman or of God in the highest sense, a concept, as they say, so high that speech turns back from it, because with the mind it cannot reach it[1]; if, as they say, it is unknown to the wise, but known to the foolish—Cognoscendo

[1] St. Augustine, De Doctr. Christ. 1, 6: 'Si autem dixi, non est quod dicere volui.'

ignoratur, Ignorando cognoscitur—how was it possible to reconcile this exalted concept with the ordinary descriptions of Brahmán, given in the Veda, nay, in some portions of these very Upanishads, as a creator, as a maker and ruler of the world; nay, often as no more than an ordinary deity?

No Esoteric Vedânta.

It has been supposed that the Vedânta consisted of two schools, an exoteric and esoteric, that the vulgar concept of Brahmán was for the former: the sublime concept for the latter. There is some truth in this, but it seems to me to import our European ideas into India. In India the truth was open to all who thirsted for it. Nothing was kept secret, no one was excluded from the temple, or rather the forest, of truth.

It is true that the lowest class, possibly the aboriginal inhabitants, were excluded. The caste of the *S*ûdras was not admitted to the education provided for the higher or the twice-born castes. To admit them to a study of the Veda would have been like admitting naked savages to the lecture-room of the Royal Institution.

And yet, in principle, even this exclusion was wrong, and clearly in contradiction with the true spirit of the Vedânta. It is generally supposed that the fourth caste, the *S*ûdras, were the aboriginal inhabitants, and racially distinct, therefore, from the Aryan conquerors. This may be so, though it has never been proved, and we know that even people of Aryan speech might lose all claim to caste, and fall socially to as low a stage as the *S*ûdras; nay, even to a lower stage. Bâdarâya*n*a speaks also of people who, owing to poverty or other circumstances, stand between the three upper castes and the *S*ûdras. And with regard to them, he distinctly states that they are not to be excluded from the study of the Vedânta. The question whether real *S*ûdras are admissible or not, has evidently exercised the minds of the Vedântists to a considerable extent, but in the end they adhere to the principle of exclusion. And yet there are cases in the Upanishads which seem to show that this spirit of exclusion was less strong in ancient times. We must not forget that in one of the hymns of the Rig-veda the *S*ûdras are distinctly stated to have sprung from Brahman like the other castes. There are not wanting indications that they spoke the same language as the Brâhmans. There are two cases, at least, in which the Upanishads seem to speak of *S*ûdras as admitted to the wisdom of the Vedânta, namely those of *G*ânas*r*uti and Satyakâma.

The story of *G*ânas*r*uti is somewhat obscure, and though *G*ânas*r*uti is distinctly called a *S*ûdra, the whole character of the story would rather seem to indicate that he was a Kshatriya, and that when Raikva called him a *S*ûdra, he used the word as a mere term of abuse. The Brâhmans themselves try by a forced etymology to show that *S*ûdra in this passage must not be taken in its technical sense, but however that may be they agree that a real *S*ûdra could not have been instructed in the Vedânta. The story runs as follows:

1. 'There lived, once upon a time, *G*ânas*r*uti Pautrâya*n*a (the great-grandson of *G*anas*r*uta), who was a pious giver, bestowing much wealth upon the people and always keeping open house. He built places of refuge everywhere, wishing

that people should everywhere eat of his food.

2. 'Once in the night some Ha*m*sas (flamingoes) flew past, and one flamingo said to the other: "He! Bhallâksha, Bhallâksha (short-sighted one), the light (glory) of *G*ânas*r*uti Pautrâya*n*a, is spread like the sky.—Do not touch it, that it may not burn thee."

3. 'The other answered him: "How can you speak of him, being what he is, as if he were like Raikva with the car[1]?"

4. 'The first replied: "How is it with this Raikva with the car of whom thou speakest?"

'The other answered: "As (in a game of dice) all the lower casts belong to him who has conquered with the K*ri*ta (the highest) cast, so whatever good deeds others perform, all belong to that Raikva with the car. He who knows what he knows, he is thus spoken of by me."

[1] The text is certainly corrupt, but none of the emendations hitherto proposed is in the least satisfactory. It is easy to say what the text ought to be, but it is difficult to explain how the text, if it ever was like what we think it ought to have been, could have become what it is now, Hic Rhodos, hic salta!

5. '*G*ânas*r*uti Pautrâya*n*a overheard this conversation, and as soon as he had risen in the morning, he said to his doorkeeper: "Thou speakest, indeed, of me as if I were Raikva with the car." He replied: "How is it with this Raikva with the car?"

6. 'The King said: "As (in a game of dice) all the lower casts belong to him who has conquered with the K*ri*ta (the highest) cast, so whatever good deeds others perform, all belong to that Raikva with the car. He who knows what he knows, is thus spoken of by me."

7. 'The doorkeeper went to look for Raikva, but returned saying, "I found him not."

'Then the King said: "Alas! where a Brâhma*n*a should be searched for (in the solitude of the forest), there go for him."

8. 'The doorkeeper came to a man who was lying beneath a car and scratching his sores. He addressed him and said: "Sir, are you Raikva with the car?"

'He answered: "Humph, I am."

'Then the doorkeeper returned and said: "I have found him."

1. 'Then *G*ânas*ruti* Pautrâya*n*a took six hundred cows, a necklace, and a carriage with mules, went to Raikva and said :

2. '" Raikva, here are six hundred cows, a necklace, and a carriage with mules; teach me the deity which you worship."

3. 'The other replied: " Fie, necklace and carriage be thine, O *S*ûdra, together with the cows!"

'Then *G*ânas*ruti* Pautrâya*n*a took again a thousand cows, a necklace, a carriage with mules, and his own daughter, and went to him.

4. 'He said to him: " Raikva, there are a thousand cows, a necklace, a carriage with mules, this wife, and this village in which thou dwellest. Sir, teach me!'

'He, lifting up her face, said: " You have brought these (cows and other presents), O *S*ûdra, but by that face (of thy daughter) alone thou wouldst have made me speak."

'These are the Raikva-par*n*a villages in the country of the Mahâv*ri*shas where Raikva dwelt under him.'

Then follows the teaching of Raikva which to

us seems hardly worthy of so large a prize as *G*ânas*r*uti offered him. The only important point in the story for our present purpose is, whether *G*ânas*r*uti was really a *S*ûdra, or whether Raikva called him a *S*ûdra in a fit of passion only. It seems to me that a man who keeps a Kshatt*ri* (doorkeeper or chamberlain), who builds towns of refuge, who can make presents of thousands of cows, bestow land on Brâhmans; lastly, who can hope that his daughter would be an acceptable gift to a Brâhman, could never have been a *S*ûdra by birth. The Vedântists, therefore, need hardly have taken so much trouble in order to explain away the case of *G*ânas*r*uti as a precedent for admitting real *S*ûdras to a study of the Upanishads and the Vedânta.

The other precedent is likewise not altogether to the point. Satyakâma is not by birth a *S*ûdra, he is the son of *G*abâlâ, who seems to have been a Brâhma*n*î by birth, but who had a son without knowing his father. Still as he and his son, when asked, both speak the truth, Gautama Hâridrumata, the teacher whom he has chosen, accepts the boy as a Brâhma*n*a and teaches him.

The story is found in the *Kh*ândogya Upanishad IV, 4:

1. Satyakâma (i.e. Philalethes), the son of *G*abâlâ, addressed his mother and said: 'I wish to become a Brahma*k*ârin (religious student), mother. Of what family am I?'

2. She said to him: 'I do not know, my child, of what family thou art. In my youth, when I had to move about much as a servant (waiting on guests in my father's house), I conceived thee. I do not know of what family thou art. I am *G*abâlâ by name, thou art Satyakâma. Say that thou art Satyakâma *G*âbâla (a member of the family of the *G*âbâlas, but here simply the son of *G*abâlâ).'

3. He, going to Gautama Hâridrumata, said to him: 'I wish to become a Brahma*k*ârin with you, Sir. May I come to you, Sir?'

4. He said to him: 'Of what family are you, my friend?' He replied: 'I do not know, Sir, of what family I am. I asked my mother, and she answered: "In my youth, when I had to move about much as a servant, I conceived thee. I do not know of what family thou art. I am

*G*abâlâ by name, thou art Satyakâma,"—I am, therefore, Satyakâma *G*âbâla, Sir.'

The teacher said to him: 'No one but a true Brâhma*n*a would thus speak out. Go and fetch fuel, friend, I shall initiate you. You have not swerved from the truth.'

These stories throw an interesting light on the state of society in the times represented by the Upanishads. But neither of them seem to me to prove what by some they were supposed to prove, namely, the right of the *S*ûdras to be taught the Vedânta. This right rested, in fact, on much higher grounds, on the ground of the common humanity of *S*ûdras and Brâhmans; but this was not recognised till Buddha proclaimed once for all that no man is a Brâhma*n*a by birth, but only by good thoughts, good words, and good deeds. But while the *S*ûdras were excluded, all the higher castes, whether Brâhma*n*as, Kshatriyas, or Vai*s*yas, were admitted to the study of the Upanishads and the Vedânta Philosophy, provided always that they had qualified themselves for these higher speculations. This insistence on certain qualifications is surely not exclusion, and no doctrine can be called *esoteric*, which is open to all who are able and willing to enter[1]. In all this, we must never forget that we are dealing with India, where, at the time when the Upanishads were composed and taught, there existed no MSS. A teacher was the depositary, the living representative of a literary composition, and it was left free to every teacher to judge whom they wished to have for their pupil, and whom they thought fit to decline. Private tutors do the same at Oxford, but no one would call their teaching *esoteric*.

We sometimes read that it is the father's duty to teach these higher doctrines to his son, and if the father's place is taken by a teacher, he is enjoined to see that his pupil is of a serene mind and endowed with all necessary qualities (Maitr. Up. VI, 29); but we never read that pupils properly qualified were excluded. We read again

[1] It has been truly said that the Gnostic tradition was secret in so far only as all Christians did not, as a matter of fact, understand it, yet not secret in so far as all ought to understand it. Hence Clement denied that the Church possessed διδαχὰς ἄλλας ἀπορρήτους, while yet he speaks of τὸ τῆς γνώμης ἀπορρητόν; cf. Bigg, Bampton Lectures on Christian Platonists, 1888, p. 57.

(*S*vet. Up. VI, 23) that this highest mystery of the Vedânta, delivered in a former age, should not be given to one whose passions have not been subdued, nor to one who is not a son or a pupil; but we have no reason to doubt that whoever was duly qualified, was duly received and duly instructed.

Relation between the Higher Bráhman and the Lower Brahmán.

With regard to the subjects taught in the Upanishads, it was the highest aim of the ancient Vedânta philosophers to show that what we might call the exoteric Brahmán was substantially the same as the esoteric, that there was in reality, and that there could be one Bráhman only, not two. The vulgar concept of Brahmán as a creator was not considered as altogether wrong. It was due, no doubt, to Nescience or Avidyâ; but it was not altogether empty or nothing; it was what we call *phenomenal*. But the Vedântists distinguished carefully between what is *phenomenal* and what is *false* or *nothing*. There is a reality behind the phenomenal world, it is not a mere nothing, as some Buddhist philosophers hold; nor is it altogether illusive, as some of the later Vedântists thought, who were therefore called Cryptobuddhists (Pra*kkh*anna-bauddhas). This is the peculiar excellence of the Vedânta philosophers, that they always see reality behind the unreal. Thus they distinguish between the qualified (sagu*n*a) and the unqualified (agu*n*a) Brahman, and they allow a qualified Brahmán for all practical purposes (vyavahâra), and more particularly for the purpose of worship (upâsanâ), because in a state of worship the human mind requires a qualified and objective God, a God the Father or the Creator, though that Father can be a person only, a pratîka or face, as the Brâhmans call it, of the Divine Substance, using the same simile of face, *persona* or person, which is well known to us from the writings of the early Fathers of the Church. Thus Brahmán may be worshipped as Î*s*vara or Lord, as a conditioned personal God, and yet be *known* as in his substance high above all conditions and limits inherent in personality. The Vedânta philosopher may even, if he likes, satisfy his craving for worship by conceiving Brahmán, as described in the Veda, as a being 'whose head is the heaven, whose eyes are sun and moon, whose breath is the wind, and whose footstool is the earth,' but he may also satisfy his rational cravings by confessing that a being, such as man is, can neither perceive nor conceive God, nor predicate anything worthy of Him. The Vedânta philosopher therefore said, 'We can only say "No, No" of God,' just as Athanasius declared (ad Monachos 2) that it is impossible to comprehend what God is, and we can only say what He is *not*. And if St. Augustine said that with regard to God, silence is better than a fight of words[1], Indian philosophy had anticipated him in this also. *S*añkara (III, 2, 27) quotes the following dialogue from an Upanishad: 'Vâshkali said: "Sir, tell me Brahman[2]." Then Bâhva became quite still. When Vâshkali had asked a second and a third time, Bâhva replied:

[1] 'Quae pugna verborum silentio cavenda magis quam voce pacanda est' (De Doctr. Christ. 1, 6).

[2] Cf. Taitt. Up. III, 1; Professor Thibaut (III, 2, 1) translates 'Learn Brahman, O friend,' which is hardly right.

"We are telling it, but thou dost not understand, that Self is quite still."' And yet this Bráhman of which the human intellect is powerless to predicate anything beyond its being, its knowing, and its being perfect or blessed, was to be worshipped by those who felt a desire for worshipping, for though it was not affected itself by any attributes, no harm would happen to the worshipper or the worshipped if he called it the Lord, the creator, the father, preserver and ruler of the world.

And what applies to Bráhman, as the Great Cause of all things, applies also to the Great Effect, namely, the Universe. Its substantial reality is not denied, for that rests on Bráhman, but all that we see and hear by our limited senses, all that we perceive and conceive and name, is purely phenomenal, as we say, is the result of Avidyâ, as the Vedântists say. The universal simile that the world is a dream turns up frequently in the Vedânta.

That what we call our real world is a world of our own making, that nothing can be long or short, black or white, bitter or sweet, apart from us, that our experience does not in fact differ from a dream, was boldly enunciated by Bishop Berkeley, of whom John Stuart Mill, no idealist by profession, declares that he was the greatest philosophical genius of all who, from the earliest times, have applied the powers of their minds to metaphysical inquiries. This is a strong testimony from such a man. 'The physical universe,' Bishop Berkeley writes, 'which I see and feel and infer, is just my dream and nothing else; that which you see, is your dream; only it so happens that our dreams agree in many respects.'

The late Professor Clifford, who likewise was no dreamer and no idealist, expressed just the same conviction when he wrote (Fortnightly Review, 1875, p. 780): 'For physical purposes a dream is just as good as real life, the only difference is in vividness and coherence.' Now what does the Vedântist say? As long as we live, he says, we dream; and our dream is real as long as we dream; but when we die, or rather when we awake and our eyes are opened by knowledge, a new world, a new reality rises before us, what Plato called the real world, of which before we knew the shadows only. This does not mean that the phenomenal world is altogether nothing,—no, it is always the effect of which Bráhman, the source of all reality, is the cause, and as, according to the Vedânta, there cannot be any substantial difference between cause and effect, the phenomenal world is substantially as real as Bráhman, nay is, in its ultimate reality, Bráhman itself.

Relation between the Higher Âtman and the Living Âtman.

We have now to follow the ancient Vedânta reasoners one step further when they fearlessly reason out their one great premiss that there is and there can be only one Bráhman, the cause of everything, that is both the material and efficient cause of everything. Nothing could exist besides Bráhman, neither matter nor souls, for if anything existed by the side of Bráhman, it would follow that Bráhman was limited, that very Bráhman which, according to its definition, is unlimited, is ekam advitîyam, one without a second. But if that is so, what does become then of the subjective soul, of the Self within us? No one could deny its existence, the Vedântist argues, for he who denies it would be the very Self that is denied, and no one can deny himself. Then what is the true Self or subject within us? or, as we should say, What is our soul? When we speak of the Self, in Sanskrit Âtman, we should always remember that it is not what is commonly meant by the Ego, but that it lies far beyond it. What we commonly call our Ego is determined by space and time, by birth and death, by the environment in which we live, by our body, our senses, our memory, by our language, nationality, character, prejudices, and many other things. All these make up our Ego, or our character, but they have nothing to do with our Self. Therefore to translate âtman by soul, as many scholars do, is rather misleading, for soul means so many things, whether the animal or living soul (*θρεπτική*), the perceptive soul (*αἰσθητική*), and the thinking soul (*νοητική*), all of which, according to the Vedânta, are perishable, non-eternal, and not the

Self. What, as we saw, Bráhman is to the world, its eternal and omnipresent cause, that the Self is to the Ego; and hence Bráhman was soon called Parama-âtman, the Highest Self, while the Self in man was called the *G*îva-âtman, for a time the living or the embodied Self.

Different Views of the Soul in Indian Philosophy.

There were philosophers in India as elsewhere, who declared that the Self or the soul was altogether nothing, or that it was the outcome of the body, or that the senses were the soul, or that the mind (manas) or our thoughts and our knowledge, were the soul. They assigned even different places in the body to the soul, just as poets imagine that the soul resides in the heart, or as lovers believe that it lives in the eyes, nay as Descartes maintained that it resided in the conarium or the pineal gland, and as many biologists still hold, that it resides in the cortical part of the brain, because it works by means of the brain. The Vedântist has therefore first of all to refute all these heretical opinions by distinguishing between what is the soul and what is not, between what is eternal, and what is perishable. No one can doubt that the body is perishable, so are, of course, our senses, so are in consequence our sensations, and what is founded on them—our percepts, our memory, our concepts, all our thoughts, all our knowledge, however profound or comprehensive. After having deducted all this, there remains no option; the individual Self must in its absolute reality be that which, according to the former argument of the Vedânta, is the All in All, the One without a Second, namely Bráhman or the Highest Self—or, as we should say, our soul *must be divine.*

But in what sense could it be the Highest Self? Some philosophers had taught that the human Self was a part of the Divine Self or a modification of it, or something created, and altogether different from it. Every one of these opinions is shown by *S*añkara to be untenable. It cannot be a part of the Divine Self, he says, for we cannot conceive parts in what is neither in time nor in space. If there existed parts of the infinite Bráhman, the Bráhman would cease to be infinite, it would be limited, and would assume a finite character as towards its parts[1]. Secondly, the living soul cannot be a modification of the Divine Self, for Bráhman, according to its very definition, is eternal and unchangeable, and as there is nothing outside of Bráhman, there is nothing that could cause a change in it. Thirdly, the living Self cannot be anything different from the Divine Self, because Bráhman, if it is anything, has to be All in All, so that there cannot be anything different from it.

Startling as the conclusion must have seemed at first, that the Divine Self and the human Self are one and the same in substance, the Vedânta philosopher did not shrink from it, but accepted it as an inevitable conclusion. The soul is God, sounds startling even to us; yet, if it is not God, what can it be? We are more accustomed to the expression that the soul is divine or God*like*, but what can be like God, if not God Himself? If Bráhman is 'one without a second,' it follows, he says, that there is no room for anything that is

[1] Spinoza, Ethica, I, Propos. XII. 'Nullum substantiae attributum potest vere concipi, ex quo sequitur substantium non posse dividi.'

not Bráhman. The often-repeated sentence, 'Tat tvam asi,' 'Thou art it,' means not that the soul is a part of Bráhman, but that the whole of Bráhman is the soul. The Vedântists were in fact what Henry More and the other Christian Platonists of Cambridge would have called *Holenmerians*, believing that the spirit is wholly present in every part (ὅλος ἐν μέρει).

The Upâdhis as the cause of difference between the Soul and God.

But then the question has to be answered, *how* Bráhman and the individual Self can be one. Bráhman or the Divine Self is eternal, omnipotent, and omnipresent, our Self clearly is not. Then why not? The answer is, 'Because it is conditioned, because it is fettered, because it is under upâdhis or *obstructions*.' It is these upâdhis or obstructions that cause the absolute Self to appear as the embodied Self (*s*arîraka). These upâdhis or obstructions are the body and its organs, the instruments of perception, conception, and of all thought, and the objective world (vishaya). We see every day that the coarse body and its members decay and perish; they, therefore, cannot be called eternal. They are objects, not the subject, they cannot constitute the eternal subject, the Self. Besides this coarse body, however, which perishes at the time of death, there is, as the Vedântists imagine, another, called the subtle body (sûkshmam *s*arîram), consisting of the vital spirits, the faculties of the senses and the manas (the mind). This subtle body is supposed to be the vehicle of the embodied soul, and the soul is supposed to dwell in it after death, till it is born again. Of course, no Indian philosopher doubts the fact of transmigration. It is to him as certain as our migration through this life. The physiological details of this migration or transmigration are often fanciful and childish. How could they be otherwise in those early days? But the broad fact of transmigration remains unaffected by these fanciful details, and it is well known that this dogma has been accepted by the greatest philosophers of all countries. Nor do these more or less fanciful details affect the broad outlines of the Vedânta system as a philosophy, for when the full truth of the Vedânta has once been grasped, transmigration also as well as the beatitudes of the heavenly paradise, vanish. When the human Self has once been known as the same as the eternal Self, there is no longer any possibility of migration, there is only peace and eternal rest in Bráhman.

The Psychology of the Vedânta.

The psychological terminology of the Vedântists may seem very imperfect and uncertain. But it has one great advantage. It does not confound soul and thought. The soul or Self has but three qualities. It is, it perceives, and it rejoices. But this perceiving of the soul is not what we mean by thinking. It is rather the light or brightness which distinguishes man from the inanimate world, which shines within, and which, when it lights up anything, is called perception or b u d d h i. In one of the Upanishads we read that men were at first stolid like stocks, till Brahman entered into them, when they became lighted up by intelligence. What we call perceiving, remembering, conceiving, imagining, and reasoning under all its forms is performed by certain instruments called the senses (indriya) and by the Manas, generally translated by mind, but really the *sensorium commune*, the rallying-point of the senses. All this, however, is not the Self. The primary instruments of all this knowledge, the sense organs, are perishable, and so is the result obtained through them, however exalted it may seem in its highest stages. The Vedântist admits five organs or senses for perception (buddhi), and five for action (karman). The former serve for the purpose of perceiving sound, shape, colour, taste, and smell, the latter for the acts of grasping, walking, speaking, and all the rest.

All sensations are conveyed by the senses to the mind, manas, the *sensorium commune* which, being either attentive or inattentive, perceives or does not perceive what is brought in. The functions of the Manas are various, such as perception (buddhi), conceptual knowledge (vi*gñ*âna), and discursive thought (*k*itta). These three functions often assume an independent character, and they then stand either in the place or by the side of the Manas. Hence much confusion in psychological terminology[1]. Other manifestations or occupations of this Manas or mind are desire (kâma)[2], imagination (saṅkalpa), doubt (vi*k*ikitsâ), faith (*s*raddhâ), want of faith (a*s*raddhâ), resolution (dh*ri*ti), irresolution (adh*ri*ti), shame (hrî), reflection (dhrî), and fear (bhî)[3]. It is difficult to find exact equivalents in English for all these technical terms. Sometimes memory would seem the best rendering of manas, mind. (Vedânta-sûtras II, 3, 32.) In fact mind or manas in the Upanishads is very comprehensive, quite as comprehensive as the Mens of Spinoza, though less defined. But though there is this want of definiteness in the Upanishads, in the first attempt to classify the various functions of the mind, *S*aṅkara, as a true monist, would himself stand up for the oneness of the mind and its ten organs,

[1] Sometimes four v*ri*ttis or activities of the inner organ are mentioned; they are mana*h* (memory or mind), buddhi (perception), aha*m*kâra (egoity), and *k*itta (thought).

[2] Cf. Spinoza, Ethica, II, vii, 3: 'Modi cogitandi, ut amor cupiditas,' &c.

[3] Also consideration (sa*ms*aya and vikalpa) and decision (ni*sk*aya and adhyâ*s*aya).

and would treat all other manifestations as so many functions (v*ri*ttis) only of one and the same mental power, called the Anta*h*-kara*n*a or the Inner Organ.

Our Mind is not our Self (Âtman).

All this may sound very imperfect, yet it contains one important thought, that our Self is neither our body nor our mind, not even our thoughts, of which most philosophers are so proud, but that all these are conditions only to which the Self has to submit, fetters by which it is chained, nay clouds by which it is darkened, so as to lose the sense of its substantial oneness with the Highest Self, and to forget the purely phenomenal character of the universe whether without or within.

The Upâdhis due to Avidyâ.

Very soon, however, a new question arose, Whence come these upâdhis or conditions, this body, these senses, this mind and all the rest? And the answer was, from Avidyâ or Nescience. Originally I believe this Nescience may have been meant as subjective only, as a confession of our inevitable ignorance of all that is transcendent, the same ignorance which has been expressed on this point with one accord by the greatest philosophers. But very soon this Avidyâ was conceived as an independent power. It was not only personal Nescience, it was universal Nescience, a Nescience not only affecting the human Self, but overshadowing for a time the Supreme Self, the very Bráhman, which, as we saw, is the substance of the human Self. Then the question would no doubt be asked once more, how can there be Nescience affecting the Supreme Self, which is All in All, subject to nothing outside it, because there *is* nothing outside it; which is therefore perfect in every way? The Vedântist can only answer that it is so. It has often been said that it is unsatisfactory for a philosopher if he has no more to say than that it is so, without being able to say, why it is so. But there is a point in every system of philosophy where a confession of ignorance is inevitable, and all the greatest philosophers have had to confess that there are limits to our understanding the world; nay, this knowledge of the limits of our understanding has, since Kant's Criticism of Pure Reason, become the very foundation of all critical philosophy. The Vedântist sees the work of Avidyâ or Nescience everywhere. He sees it in our not knowing our own true nature, and in our believing in the objective world as it appears and disappears. He guards against calling this universal Avidyâ *real*, in the sense in which Bráhman is real, yet he cannot call it altogether unreal, because it has at all events caused all that seems to be real, though it is itself unreal. Its only reality consists in the fact that it has to be assumed, and that there is no other assumption possible to account for what is called the real world. To know what this Nescience or Avidyâ is, is impossible, nay, self-contradictory. And to this effect a very telling verse is quoted, namely, that he who would know Avidyâ is like a man who should wish to see darkness by means of a far-shining torch [1].

[1] This view of Nescience or Avidyâ is clearly put forward in the Vedântasiddhântamuktâvalî as translated by Professor Venis (pp. 14–15): 'Of the reality of Nescience (avidyâ) there is no

Avidyâ destroyed by Knowledge.

But while for a time this Nescience has power to conquer and enslave us, we have the power in the end by means of true Science (Vidyâ) to conquer and enslave it, nay to destroy it and all its works; and this true Science, this Vidyâ, is the *Vedânta philosophy*. It is true we cannot shake off our fetters, but we can know them to be but fetters; we cannot rid ourselves of our body and its senses or destroy the phenomenal world, but we can soar above it and watch it till it stops. This is called freedom even in this life (*g*ivanmukti), which becomes perfect freedom at the time of death. The Vedânta philosopher has

evidence, revealed or human. . . . Is Nescience proved by Veda or by perception, &c., or is it assumed to account for the world of experience, which cannot otherwise be accounted for? Not by Veda, nor by perception, inference, or human teaching. For, if by any of these Nescience were clearly proved, controversy would be at an end. And since there is no evidence for Nescience it must needs be granted that Nescience is *assumed* to account for the otherwise inexplicable production of the unreal world. . . . For there is no other course apart from this assumption of Nescience.' See Col. Jacob, Vedânta-sâra, p. 173.

a simile for everything. The potter's wheel, he says, goes on revolving, even after the impetus given to it has ceased. And in the same way our phenomenal life goes on, though its impetus, namely Avidyâ or Nescience, has been destroyed. The last word in this life, the last word of the Vedânta philosophy is Tat tvam asi, *Thou art it*, or Aham brahmâsmi, *I am Bráhman*. 'With this,' we are told, 'the fetters of the heart are broken, all doubts are rent asunder; all works are destroyed, for the Eternal (Bráhman), the highest and the lowest, has been seen.'

Bhidyate h*ri*dayagranthi*h*
*Kh*idyante sarvasa*m*sayâ*h*,
Kshîyante *k*âsya karmâ*n*i
Tasmin d*ri*sh*t*e parâvare.

Let me read you in conclusion another short chapter of *S*ankara's (IV, 1, 2), in which he tries to explain in what sense our Self can be the Highest Self, and how the soul can have its true being in God and in God only.

How the Soul can be one with God.

*S*aṅkara says: 'The author of the Sûtras considers whether the Âtman, the Self, is to be accepted as I, or as something different from the I. And if it is said, how can there be a doubt, considering that the word Âtman occurs in the Veda in the sense of the inward Self or the I?—the answer is that this word Âtman may be taken in this its original sense, provided it is possible to take the living soul and the Lord as not different from one another; but, if not, then, and then only, the word might be taken in its secondary sense.' Hence the usual opponent is introduced as saying: 'It cannot be taken in the primary sense of I, for he who possesses the qualities of sinlessness, &c., i.e. the Lord, cannot be comprehended as possessing the opposite qualities (sin, &c.), nor *vice versâ*. Now the Highest Lord is sinless, the embodied Self on the contrary is sinful. Again, if the Lord were immersed in sa*m*sâra (migration) or a temporary being, he would *ipso facto* not be the Lord, and hence the Scripture would lose its meaning. Again, supposing that the temporary Self could be the Self of the Lord, the Scripture would be meaningless, because there would be no one qualified (to study the Vedânta and to recover Brahmahood), nay the very evidence of the senses would be contradicted. And if it should be said, granted that the two are different, and that the Scripture teaches that we must consider them as one, why not admit that they may then be taken as one in the same sense in which Vish*n*u is taken as one with his images? This surely would be better than to admit that the temporal soul is the chief Lord himself. This is our opinion:' i.e. these are the objections that can be made, if only for the sake of argument, against the other, the true position. Against all this *we* say—that is the real *S*ankara says: that the temporal self *is* the same as the Self of the Lord[1].

'The Highest Lord is to be understood as the

[1] Professor Thibaut (Introd. p. 100) and Col. Jacob seem to hold that this identity of the individual and the highest Self is not to be ascribed to Bâdarâya*n*a. Jacob, Vedânta-sâra, p. iv. It is, however, the doctrine of the Upanishads.

Self (in us), for in treating of the Highest Lord the *G*âbâlas take Him as the Self (in us), saying, "Indeed I am thou, O holy Deity, and thou art I, O Deity." And to the same effect other passages also, such as "I am Brahman," are to be considered as teaching that the Lord is the Self (within). There are Vedânta-texts teaching that the Lord is the Self (within), for instance: "This is thy Self which is within all;" "He is thy Self, the inward ruler, the immortal;" "that is the True, that is the Self, and thou art it," &c. And when it was suggested that what is contended for is a symbolic likeness only, as in the case of the images of Vish*n*u, this is altogether out of place, for it is objectionable as farfetched (secondary); nay the construction of the sentences also is against it. For when the perception of a symbolic likeness is intended, the word is used once, for instance, "Brahman is Mind," "Brahman is Âditya (the sun)." But in our text it is said, "I am thou, thou art I." Therefore on account of the difference of the scripture-wording, we must accept non-difference (between the Lord and the Self). Besides, there is a distinct denial of difference in the Veda. For it says: "Whoever worships another god, thinking, He is one, and I am another, he does not know" (B*ri*h. Âr. Upan. I, 4, 10); "He goes from death to death who sees diversity here" (B*ri*h. IV, 4, 19); and again, "Whosoever looks for anything elsewhere than in the Self, is abandoned by everything" (B*ri*h. II, 4, 6). This and further passages of the Veda contradict the view of difference (between the personal and the Highest Self).

'And with regard to what was said of contradictory qualities being impossible in the Self, that is no real objection, for it has been shown to be wrong to admit contradictory qualities. Further, when it was said that in that case there would be no Lord, this is wrong again, for there is the authority of Scripture for it, nor do we ourselves understand it in that sense. For we do not understand that the Lord is the temporal Self, but what we wish to establish is that the temporal Self, if divested of its temporal character, is the Self of the Lord. This being so, it follows that the non-dual Lord is sinless, and that the opposite quality (sinfulness) would be ascribed to him by mistake.

'And as to there being no qualified person (for studying the Vedânta), or the very evidence of the senses being against us, that again is wrong. For before the enlightenment takes place, we fully admit the temporal character of the Self, and the evidence of the senses has reference to that character only, while the passage, "If the Self only were all this, how would he see anything?" shows that as soon as enlightenment takes place, the action of the senses comes to an end. The objection that on the ceasing of sensuous perception the Scripture also would cease, is nothing; nay we ourselves approve of it, because, according to the passage beginning with "Then the father is no father," and ending with "Then the Vedas are no Vedas," we ourselves admit that with enlightenment Scripture ceases. And if you ask, "Who is not enlightened?" we say, "You yourself who can ask such a question." And if you say, "But am I not by the very Scripture declared to be the Lord?" we reply, "Yes, you are, but if you are enlightened so far, then nobody is unenlightened." The same answer applies to the objection started by some, that there cannot be non-duality of the Self, because through Avidyâ (Nescience) the Self has a second, that is to say before enlightenment takes place. The final result is that we should think of the Self within us as the Lord.'

All this, we must always remember, is not meant as an apotheosis of man in the Greek sense of the word, but, if I may form such a word, as an *Anatheosis*, a return of man into the divine nature. The German Mystics have clearly distinguished between these two acts, by calling the former *Vergötterung*, the latter *Vergottung*; and while they would consider the former as blasphemous, they look upon the latter as only another expression for divine sonship, the highest aim of the religion of Christ.

LECTURE III.

SIMILARITIES AND DIFFERENCES BETWEEN INDIAN AND EUROPEAN PHILOSOPHY.

Strangeness of Eastern Philosophy.

THE account which I am able to give you of the ancient Vedânta philosophy in the short space of two or three lectures, is naturally very imperfect, and confined to its most salient features only. It would have been equally difficult to give within such narrow limits a general idea of any complete system of philosophy, whether of Plato or Kant, though with regard to these we move on more or less familiar ground, nay, we are acquainted, even without any special study, with some of their terminology at least. It forms part of our unconscious education to know the difference between *spirit* and *matter*, between *genus* and *species*, nay, we often talk of *specific* differences without being aware that *specific* is simply what makes a species, a Latin translation of the Greek εἰδοποιός, that is, some characteristic mark which makes a new εἶδος or species, and thus constitutes the difference between one species and another. We talk of *ideas*, innate or acquired, of *categories*, nay even of *pure reason* long before we know what they really mean. But a system of Indian philosophy is like a strange Eastern city, of which we know neither the streets nor the names of the streets, and where we are in constant danger of going wrong, even with a Murray and a map in our hands to guide us. The very grooves of thought are different in the East and in the West. It would by no means be easy to find in Sanskrit corresponding terms to express the exact difference between matter and spirit from the Vedântic point of view. The nearest approach would probably be *object* and *subject*, and this would be expressed by vishaya, object, and vishayin, he who perceives an object, that is, the subject. If we had to translate *idea*, we should probably have to use such a word as sa*m*g*ñ*a, which means *name*, the outward form of an idea. *Category* is generally and correctly rendered in Sanskrit by padârtha, but padârtha really means the object or the meaning of a word. Hence it could be used to express the general predicates, that is, the categories, such as substance, quality, and all the rest; but Sanskrit is so philosophical a language that it uses padârtha in the ordinary sense of *thing* also, as if the framers of that language had known that to us a thing is no more than *a think*—the meaning, the intention, or the object of a word. Even such familiar terms as religion and philosophy are by no means easy to render into Sanskrit, because the Indian mind does not look upon them as standing in the same relation to each other in which they seem to us to stand.

In one sense, therefore, it is quite true that in order to understand Indian philosophy we must learn to understand Indian language.

General Interest of Indian Philosophy.

However, in inviting you to listen to these short lectures on the ancient Vedânta philosophy, my only object was to convince you that this ancient city of philosophic thought, the Vedânta, was worth a visit, nay, if you have the time, worth a careful exploration, such as an intelligent traveller can afford in a journey through the magnificent temples and tombs of ancient thought. It is something to have seen Karnak, even if we are unable to read all the hieroglyphic inscriptions on its walls. It is something to have seen the deep foundations and the sublime structures of the Vedânta philosophy, even though there was no time to explore all its passages, and to ascend its highest watch-towers.

When after the fall of Constantinople the West of Europe became once more acquainted with the original texts of Greek philosophy, life seemed to grow richer in the West by the ancient treasures of thought that had been brought to light in the East. The discovery of Indian literature, and more particularly of Indian religion and philosophy, was likewise the recovery of an old, and the discovery of a new world; and even if we can throw but a passing glance at the treasures of ancient thought which are stored up in Sanskrit literature, we feel that the world to which we belong has grown richer, nay, we feel proud of the unexpected inheritance in which all of us may share.

Only let us avoid that fatal superciliousness which turns away from all that seems strange, and despises all that it cannot at once understand. We may smile at much of what the thinkers of ancient Greece and India have left us, but we need not sneer. I am no promiscuous admirer of everything that comes from the East. I have again and again expressed my regret that the Sacred Books of the East contain so much of what must seem to us mere rubbish, but that should not prevent us from appreciating what is really valuable in them.

Critical Treatment of Oriental Literature.

I know I have often been blamed for calling rubbish what to the Indian mind seemed to contain profound wisdom, and to deserve the highest respect. I strongly hold that we ought always to speak cautiously and respectfully where religion is concerned, and I am quite willing to admit that on religious questions it is often very difficult to place ourselves in exactly the same position which the Oriental mind has occupied for centuries. We all know from our own experience that what has been handed down to us as very ancient, and what as children we have been taught to consider as sacred, retains through life a fascination which it is difficult to shake off altogether. Every attempt to discover reason in what is unreasonable is accepted as legitimate so long as it enables us to keep what we are unwilling to part with. Still it cannot be denied that the Sacred Books of the East are full of rubbish, and that the same stream which carries down fragments of pure gold, carries also sand and mud and much that is dead and offensive. That many things which occur in the hymns of the Veda, in the Brâhma*n*as, and in the Upanishads also, struck even an Oriental mind as so much rubbish, accumulated, we hardly know how, in the course of centuries, we may learn from Buddha. His hostility towards the Brâhmans has been very much exaggerated, and we know by this time that most of his doctrines were really those of the Upanishads. But though he would take and retain the gold in the ancient literature of India, he would not accept the rubbish. Buddha's words on this subject deserve to be quoted, not only as showing that to an Oriental mind much that the Brâhmans called venerable and inspired, seemed useless and absurd, but at the same time as exhibiting a freedom of judgement which we ourselves find it often difficult to maintain. In the Kalama Sutta Buddha says: 'Do not believe in what ye have heard; do not believe in traditions because they have been handed down for many generations; do not believe in anything because it is rumoured and spoken of by many; do not believe merely because the written statement of some old sage is produced; do not believe in conjectures; do not believe in that as truth to which you have become attached by habit; do not believe merely on the authority of your teachers and elders;—after observation and analysis, when it agrees with reason and is conducive to the good and benefit of one and all, then accept it and live up to it' (Aṅguttara Nikâya, quoted in Transact. of the Parl. of Rel., vol. ii. p. 869). It required courage to say this in India, it requires courage to say it at any time, but it shows at all events that even an Oriental mind could not bring himself to admire all that had been handed down as ancient and sacred. Here is an example which we ought to follow, always trying to separate the wheat from the chaff, to prove all things, and to hold fast that which is good. Now I say again there is plenty of wheat in the Veda, particularly in the Upanishads, but there is also plenty of chaff, and in answer to my critics I may say that it is not likely that anybody can truly appreciate the wheat, who cannot also reject the chaff.

The Sacred Syllable Om.

Much, for instance, that is said in the Upanishads about the sacred syllable Om, seems to my mind mere twaddle, at least in its present form. I cannot bring myself to give specimens, but you have only to read the beginning of the *Kh*ândogya Upanishad, and you will see what I mean. It is quite possible that originally there was some sense in all the nonsense that we find in the Upanishads about the sacred syllable Om. This Om may originally have had a meaning, it may be a contraction of a former *avam, and this avam may have been a prehistoric pronominal stem, pointing to distant objects, while ayam pointed to nearer objects. In that case, avam may have become the affirmative particle om, just as the French *oui* arose from *hoc illud.* And thus we read in the *Kh*ândogya Upanishad I, 1, 8: 'That syllable is a syllable of permission, for whenever we permit anything we say Om, yes.' If, then, om meant originally that and *yes*, we can understand that, like *Amen*, it may have assumed a more general meaning, something like tat sat, and that it may have been used as representing all that human language can express. Thus in the Maitrâya*n*a Upanishad VI, 23, after it had been said there was one Brahman without words, and a second, a Word-Brahman, we are told that the word is the syllable Om. This sounds absurd, unless we admit that this Om was meant at first as a symbol of all speech, even as a preacher might say that all language was Amen, Amen.

Whatever was Old became Sacred.

It is indeed very difficult to account for this strange mixture of wisdom and folly even in the Veda, more particularly in the Brâhma*n*as, except by supposing that at the time when these ancient compositions were reduced to writing, anything that had been handed down as old, was considered sacred and worthy of being preserved. We ought to remember what hideous and decayed things our own antiquarian friends are able to admire, simply because they are *molto antico.* Nor should it be forgotten that a long-continued oral tradition by which the Veda had been handed down from generation to generation, before it was written, may likewise account for the creeping in of a large amount of epigonic thought. We see the same admixture in the Homeric poems (for even Homer is sometimes drowsy), and likewise in the popular poetry of other nations, whether Scandinavians or Germans, of Fins or Laps. But admitting all this, is it not the duty of the historian to do what gold-washers have to do, and not to mind the muddy water, and the clay, and the sand, if only some grains of genuine gold can be recovered in the end?

I did not expect that any of my hearers would join the gold-washers, would begin the study of Sanskrit in order to be able to read the Upanishads and the Vedânta-sûtras in the original. I only wished them to look at some of the gold-dust and some of the large nuggets, in order that in future the map of India, from the Himalayan mountains to Cape Comorin, should in their minds be coloured, not grey and black, but bright and golden.

Sanskrit is not the difficult language which it is generally supposed to be. I know of several ladies who have learnt it very well; I know of one Professor of Philosophy at least who has considered it his duty to learn Sanskrit in order to study the different systems of Indian philosophy.

Books for the Study of the Vedânta.

The Upanishads and the Vedânta-sûtras belong certainly to the most difficult works to translate from Sanskrit into any modern language, whether English or German. We are constantly made aware of our deficiencies in being unable to catch and to render accurately the minute shades of meaning, whether of the inspired seers of the Upanishads, or the acute reasoners of the Vedânta school of philosophy. Again and again, though we may clearly perceive the drift of the original, we find it almost impossible to give a close and faithful equivalent in English. However, I have ventured on an English translation of all the important Upanishads, and have published it in the first and fifteenth volumes of my Sacred Books of the East. In cases where some of these Upanishads had been translated before, I have often had to differ from my predecessors, and of course there have not been wanting critics who have differed from me. In several cases their criticisms have proved useful, in others they seemed to me so ignorant and unscholarlike as to deserve no notice, much less a refutation. Still I have no doubt that future translators will find plenty of work to do, particularly if they allow themselves to have recourse to conjectural emendations of the text. In a first attempt I thought it right to avoid as much as possible any conjectural alterations of the Sanskrit text, particularly when that text is confirmed by the commentary of *S*aṅkara, written not later than 800 A. D.; for we possess no MSS. of the Upanishads of anything like that age. I also thought it right to follow the guidance of *S*aṅkara as much as possible, and never to deviate from him except where his interpretation could be clearly shown to be wrong or artificial, and where a better interpretation could be supported by valid arguments. These principles which I followed in my translation may not recommend themselves to all scholars, but I am glad to find that the translators of *S*aṅkara's Commentary on the Vedânta-sûtras, and other scholars really competent to judge, have approved of them, and have found my translation both trustworthy and serviceable.

There is also a most excellent translation of the Vedânta-sûtras with *S*aṅkara's commentary in the thirty-fourth and thirty-eighth volumes of the same collection, contributed by Professor Thibaut, who is resident in the very centres of Vedânta learning, at Benares and Allahabad. There is a German translation of the same work by Professor Deussen, Professor of Philosophy in the University of Kiel, the German professor who did not shrink from the trouble of learning Sanskrit with the sole object of studying this Vedânta philosophy, of which Schopenhauer, as you may remember, had spoken in such glowing terms. This translation made by a well-schooled philosopher, will show at all events that a man deeply versed in Plato, Aristotle, Spinoza, and Kant, did not think it a waste of time to devote some of the best years of his life to the Vedânta, nay to make a journey to India, in order to come into personal contact with the still living representatives of the Vedânta philosophy. This may possibly serve to convince those who are always sceptical as to any good thing coming out of India, that even our philosophy may have something to learn from ancient Indian philosophy. Still it would not be honest on my part were I not to tell you that while German philosophers of the calibre of Schopenhauer, Deussen, and others, expect from this study almost as great a revival in philosophy, as a study of Sanskrit and the religion and mythology of India has produced in comparative philology, theology, and mythology, there have not been wanting others who look upon the Vedânta philosophy as mere twaddle, and as utterly unworthy of the attention of serious students of philosophy. You should hear both sides and judge for yourselves. Only you should remember that there is no philosophy which has not been called 'mere twaddle' by some one more wise than the wisest. In the eyes of some people all philosophy is twaddle, or even madness, while others call it a 'divine madness.'

There are some other valuable books, such as the translation of the more modern Vedânta-sâra by Colonel Jacob, and some more texts translated by Professor Venis in the volumes of the 'Pandit.' Colebrooke's Essays on Indian Philosophy, though written long ago, are still very instructive, and Professor Gough's Essays on the Upanishads deserve careful consideration, though we may differ from the spirit in which they are written. The same remark applies to a work called 'A Rational Refutation of the Hindu Philosophical Systems,' by my old friend Nîlaka*nth*a *S*âstrî Ghore (a convert to Christianity and a Missionary at Poona), translated from Hindi into English by Dr. Fitz-Edward Hall, Calcutta, 1862, a learned and honest work, though written in a decidedly controversial spirit.

Coincidences. Spinoza's 'Substantia.'

Strange as this Vedânta philosophy must appear at first sight to most of us, you can hardly have failed to discover some striking similarities which it presents with the great systems of European philosophy. Thus the Brahman, as conceived in the Upanishads and defined by *S*ankara, is clearly the same as Spinoza's 'Substantia.' Spinoza defines it as that which is in itself and is conceived by itself (in se est and per se concipitur). It is according to him infinite, indivisible, one, free and eternal, just as *S*ankara's Bráhman is called in the Upanishads 'unborn, undecaying, undying, without parts, without action, tranquil, without fault or taint.' But while with Spinoza this 'Substantia' simply takes the place of God[1], *S*añkara, when asked whether Bráhman is God, would have to answer both Yes and No. No doubt, he defines Bráhman as 'the omniscient and omnipotent cause of the origin, the permanence, and the disappearance of the world;' but as he distinguishes between a phenomenal and a real world, he distinguishes likewise between a phenomenal and a real God. This is a very important distinction. There is, he says, a lower and a higher Brahman. Even the lower one is adorned with the highest predicates which human language has to bestow; but the higher one is above all praise and all predicates; even the highest which other religions have bestowed on the Deity are unworthy of Bráhman. According to *S*añkara God, as conceived by the many, as an historical person, who some hundreds or some thousands of years ago created the world and remained its permanent ruler, is phenomenal only, that is to say, he *is* the real Bráhman, but

[1] Per Deum intelligo ens absolute infinitum, hoc est, substantiam constantem infinitis attributis, quorum unumquodque aeternam essentiam exprimit.

hidden behind the veil of human Nescience or Avidyâ. This may seem at first sight a very low idea of God, but, if properly understood, it is really the highest and truest view that can be taken. For phenomenal does not mean what is altogether false and unreal; the phenomenal God is the most real God, only as conceived by the human understanding, which never can form an adequate idea of the Deity, because the Deity is inconceivable and ineffable. For all practical purposes, however, for the purposes of religion and morality, that phenomenal Deity is all that can be required. It is for philosophers only, for the Vedântist, that a higher reality is required, and this both for the subjective Bráhman, and for the objective world. The phenomenal reality of the objective world lasts as long as the conditions of the subject and the object of experience remain what they are. To those who cannot see a higher reality behind the phenomenal world, the phenomenal world possesses, of course, the most absolute reality, while in their eyes the real world postulated by the philosopher behind the veil of the senses, is utterly unreal, is pure imagination.

The Vedântist is quite satisfied that it should be so; he has no hard names for those who believe in a phenomenal world and a phenomenal God. He knows that the time will come when their eyes are opened, and till then, though they worship God ignorantly, still they worship God, the *real* God or Bráhman.

The Meanings of Real.

Few words have so many meanings as *real*, few words have undergone so many violent changes of meaning. Still for every honest thinker there is and there can be one reality only. Nor can we call anything unreal unless we know something that is real, and *vice versâ*. Thus to the great majority of mankind, what we call the phenomenal world is thoroughly real, they know nothing more real; what the Vedântist calls the phenomenal God, the Lord or Î*s*vara, is to them the only real and true God[1]. But the time

[1] The same idea is expressed in somewhat involved language by a modern philosopher, as follows: 'Reality under the forms of our consciousness is and can only be the conditioned effect of the absolute reality; but this conditioned effect stands in

comes when it is perceived that the phenomenal world is but phenomenal, and the phenomenal Deity is but phenomenal, and that behind these appearances there must be something real that appears. This is what the Vedânta calls the true Bráhman, the Highest Self, the really real God. That Bráhman, as *S*ankara says, though ignorantly worshipped, remains unaffected by our inadequate conceptions. He is not tainted by our ignorance, as little as the sun is tainted by the clouds that pass over it. Nay, we may learn in time that as the human eye cannot see the sun, except when covered by those passing clouds, the human mind also cannot possibly conceive God except behind the veil of human language and human thought. The phenomenal Brahmán is therefore nothing but the real Bráhman, only veiled in time by Nescience or Avidyâ.

---

indissoluble relation with its unconditioned cause, and being equally persistent with it, so long as the conditions persist, is to consciousness supplying these conditions, equally real.' (Theosophy, p. 322.) See also Deussen, System des Vedânta, p. 59, note.

The Nature of Avidyâ and Mâyâ.

That Avidyâ, however, is not meant for our own individual ignorance, but as an ignorance inherent in human nature, nay as something like a general cosmical force, as darkness inevitable in the light, which causes the phenomenal world to seem and to be to us what it seems and what it is. Hence this Nescience or Avidyâ came to be called 'Mâyâ,' originally power (also *S*akti), the productive cause of the whole world. This Mâyâ soon assumed the meaning of Illusion, Deception, Fraud, nay it assumed a kind of mythological personality. The whole of this development of Vedântic thoughts, however, is certainly late, and whatever may have been written against it, Colebrooke, I think, was perfectly right when he said 'that the notion that the versatile world is an entire illusion (Mâyâ), and that all that passes to the apprehension of the waking individual is but a phantasy, presented to his imagination, nay that every seeming thing is unreal, and all is visionary, does not appear to be the doctrine of the text of the Vedânta.'

Colebrooke on Mâyâ.

Those who boldly maintained that Colebrooke was wrong 'from first to last,' seem hardly to have understood Colebrooke's meaning. Let us look at the facts first. The very word Mâyâ never occurs in the principal Upanishads in the same sense as Avidyâ. It begins to show in the *S*vetâ*s*vatara Upanishad, which held a position of its own. This is surely an important fact, and as we now possess Colonel Jacob's Concordance, we can assert it with perfect confidence. When Mâyâ occurs once in the plural, in the B*ri*had Âr. Upanishad II, 5, 19, this is really a quotation from the Rig-veda VI, 47, 18, and shows how Mâyâ, in the sense of *S*akti, power, came to find its way into the language of the Vedânta. In compound words also, Mâyâ generally means power, creative power, very much like *S*akti, though in some of the later Upanishads it has taken the place of Avidyâ. The Vedânta warns us again and again that we must distinguish between two kinds of illusion. When we imagine we see a serpent instead of a rope, there is something real behind the illusion, but when a man in an access of fever imagines he sees a devil, there is nothing real, no real devil, no devil *an sich*, behind it. This idea, that the world is only Mâyâ, an illusion, a vision, a nothing, was what Colebrooke meant when he said it was absent from the Upanishads and the original Vedânta philosophy, and so far he is right. The idea that the world is nothing but Mâyâ or illusion is a view which *S*añkara mentions as the theory of the Buddhists or the *S*ûnyavâdins, that is, of those who say that everything is emptiness.

It is true that some of the Vedântists also, who are therefore called Crypto-buddhists, failed to distinguish between what is absolutely and what is relatively real. But the true Vedântists always held that behind the relatively real there was the absolutely real, that behind the phenomenal world there was the full reality of Bráhman, and that in believing and ignorantly worshipping a Maker of the world, an individual Deity, not entirely divested of all human qualities, they were believing and worshipping the true

God, the eternal Bráhman, the inconceivable and inexpressible source of all things.

Sir W. Jones on the Vedânta.

Sir William Jones also perceived, like Colebrooke, the true character of the ancient Vedânta when he wrote: 'The fundamental tenet of the Vedânta school consisted not in denying the existence of matter, that is, of solidity, impenetrability and extended figure (to deny which would be lunacy), but in correcting the popular notion of it, and in contending that it has no essence independent of mental perception, that existence and perceptibility are convertible terms, that external appearances and sensations are illusory, and would vanish into nothing, if the divine energy, which alone sustains them, were suspended but for a moment; an opinion Epicharmus and Plato seem to have adopted, and which has been maintained in the present century with great elegance, but with little public applause, partly because it has been misunderstood, and partly because it has been misapplied by the false reasoning of some unpopular writers, who are said to have disbelieved in the moral attributes of God, whose omnipresence, wisdom, and goodness are the basis of Indian philosophy' (Works, i. pp. 20, 125, 127).

This fact, this perception of a relative truth contained in our phenomenal experience, explains, I believe, why we find in the Vedânta philosophy the same tolerant spirit which we find generally in Indian religion. As the Supreme Spirit is made to say in the Bhagavadgîtâ, 'Even those who worship idols, worship me,' Bráhman might say in the Vedânta philosophy, 'Even those who worship a personal God under the image of an active workman, or a King of kings, worship, or, at all events, mean, me.'

This is a very important distinction both from a philosophical and from a religious point of view.

The Two Brahmans are One.

We can well understand that when the same word Brahman was applied in two such different senses, as the High and as the Low Brahman, as an unconditioned and as a conditioned being, there must have been great danger of frequent misunderstandings, and *S*ankara had, therefore, to devote a considerable portion of his work to showing in numerous passages of the Upanishads which of the two ideas was present in each case to the thought of their authors. At last he asks himself (IV, 3, 14): 'What then,—are there two Brahmans, a higher and a lower?' And he answers, 'Indeed, there are two.' And thus we read in one Upanishad (Pra*s*na V, 2): 'The syllable Om is the higher and also the other Brahman. What then is the higher Bráhman, and what the other Brahmán?' He answers, When Bráhman is described in the Upanishads by negative words only, after excluding all differences of name and form, due to Nescience—that is the Higher. But when he is described by such terms as (*Kh*ând. III, 14, 2), 'the intelligent whose body consists of spirit, whose body is light, being distinguished by some special name and form, for the sake of worship only, that is the other, the lower, Brahmán.'

But if that be so, then the text saying that Bráhman has no second (*Kh*ând. VI, 2, 1) would seem to be contradicted. 'No,' he says, 'it would not, because all this is only the illusion of name and form, produced by Nescience.' In reality the two Brahmans are one and the same Brahman—the one conceivable, the other inconceivable; the one phenomenal, the other absolutely real.

Nothing can be clearer than the distinction here drawn by *S*aṅkara. With the poets of the Upanishads, however, the line between the Higher and the other Brahmán was not always so sharply drawn, and here *S*aṅkara has often to explain and sometimes to twist the natural sense of the Upanishads. Thus, when interpreting the numerous passages of the Upanishads which describe the return of the human soul after death to Brahmán, *S*aṅkara always takes Brahmán as the conditioned or the Low Brahmán. 'For a human soul,' he says, 'which has found the knowledge of the Highest Bráhman cannot die, cannot be moving towards Bráhman.' That soul, as *S*aṅkara boldly expresses it, 'becomes Bráhman by being Bráhman,' that is, by knowing himself, by knowing what he is, and always has been. Remove Nescience and there is light, and in that light the human Self and the Divine Self shine forth in their eternal oneness. From this point of view of the highest reality, there is no difference between the highest Bráhman and the individual Self or Âtman (Ved.-sûtras I, 4, 1, p. 339). The body, with all the conditions or upâdhis attached to it, may continue for a time, even after the light of knowledge has appeared, but death will come and bring immediate freedom and perfect blessedness; while those who, thanks to their good works, may enter the celestial paradise, have to wait even there, till they obtain the highest enlightenment, and are then only restored to their true nature, their true liberty, that is, their true oneness with Bráhman.

The Germs of the Vedânta in the Upanishads.

When we consider how abstruse many of these metaphysical ideas are which form the substance of the Vedânta philosophy, it is most interesting to see how *S*aṅkara succeeds in discovering them all, or at all events their germs, in the ancient Upanishads. It is true he sometimes reminds us of the manner in which texts of the Bible used to be interpreted, or, as it was called, 'improved,' in academic sermons. And yet we cannot deny that the germs of many of the most recondite thoughts of Vedânta metaphysicians are really there, imbedded in the Upanishads. Of course, there is as yet no strict and consistent terminology in those ancient texts, and their method is assertive rather than argumentative. The prevalent conception of Brahmán, for instance, is certainly mythological in the Upanishads. He is not only the germ of golden light (Hira*n*yagarbha), he is seen within the sun with golden beard and golden hair, golden altogether to the very tips of his nails, and his eyes are blue like lotus-flowers (*Kh*ând. I, 6, 6). Yet, in *S*añkara's eyes, all this is only the phenomenal outside of the real Bráhman, and of Him the same Upanishads say, 'Truly, O friend, this Imperishable is neither coarse nor fine[1], neither short nor long, neither red (like fire) nor fluid (like water); it is without shadow, without darkness, without air, without ether, without attachment, without eyes, without ears, without speech, without mind, without light, without breath, without a mouth, without measure,

[1] B*ri*h. Âr. III, 8, 8.

having no within and no without [1].' And this process of negation, or what may truly be called abstraction, goes on, till every leaf of the flower is plucked off, and nothing remains but the calyx or the seed, the inconceivable Bráhman, the Self of the world. 'He sees, but is unseen; he hears, but is unheard; he perceives, but is unperceived; nay, there is nothing in the world that sees, or hears, or perceives, or knows, but Bráhman alone.'

If it is said in the Upanishads that Bráhman is the light in the sun, the Vedântist should learn to understand that it is so, for what else could that light be but Bráhman, which is all in all. Though we should not say that Bráhman in its entirety is the light, the light in its entirety is Bráhman. The nearest approach which metaphysical language can make to Bráhman, is to call it Light, as it were, conscious light, which would be another name for knowledge. And so we read in the Mu*nd*aka Upanishad (V, 2): 'This is the light of lights; when it shines, the sun does not shine, nor the moon and the stars, nor lightnings, much less this fire. When Bráhman

[1] Deussen, System, p. 146; Sûtras I, 1, 5.

shines, everything shines after him, by his light all the world is lighted.' Conscious light would best represent the knowledge ascribed to Bráhman, and it is well known that *Thomas Aquinas*[1] also called God the intelligent Sun (*Sol intelligibilis*). For though all purely human attributes are withheld from Bráhman, knowledge, though knowledge without external objects, is left to Him.

The Knowledge of Brahman.

Knowledge is in fact the only human predicate which all religions venture to ascribe to the Supreme Being; though, in doing so, they often forget what an imperfect thing human knowledge is, even when it has reached its highest perfection, and how unworthy the Deity, even in its utmost grandeur. There is a passive element in all human knowledge, and this would be incompatible with Deity. The Vedânta calls Bráhman omniscient, but another system of philosophy, the Sâṅkhya, objects to this as too anthropomorphic. The Sâṅkhya philosophers argue, 'If you ascribe

[1] S. Th. I, 2, qu. 109, art. 1, ad 2.

omniscience, that is, a necessary knowledge of all things, to Bráhman, you make him dependent on the objects, with reference to the act of knowing; he cannot help knowing, just as we cannot help seeing, even if we do not like it; and this would be unworthy of Bráhman.' This, no doubt, is a very subtle objection, but the Vedântist meets it boldly and says: 'The sun also, although his heat and light are permanent, is nevertheless designated as independent, when we say, "he shines, he warms."' The Sâṅkhya philosopher, however, does not yield yet. 'The sun,' he replies, 'must have objects to light and to warm, whereas before the creation of the world, there could not have been any objects on which Bráhman could shine, which he could have seen or known.' And here the reply of the Vedântist becomes very important. 'First of all,' he says, 'the sun would shine, even if it had nothing to shine on. But, apart from that, Bráhman was before the creation of the world, and had always something to know and think upon.'

Names and Forms, as the Objects of Brahmán's Knowledge.

If we ask what the objects of his eternal thoughts could have been, the Vedântist answers: 'Names and forms' (nâma-rûpe). You will perceive at once the extraordinary similarity between this theory, and the Platonic theory of the ideas, and more still the Stoic theory of the *Logos*, language and thought. That thought and language are inseparable, had been clearly perceived by the Stoic and Platonist philosophers at Alexandria, when calling the creative ideas of the Deity logoi, that is both words and thoughts; and equally so by the ancient Hindu philosophers when they called the same thoughts nâma-rûpe, names and forms. These names and forms are, in fact, the εἴδη or ideas of Plato, and the species of the later Stoics[1]. As thought by Brahman, before the creation of the world, these name-forms were non-manifest (avyâk*ri*ta); in the created world they are manifest (vyâk*ri*ta), and manifold.

[1] The Buddhists call them sa*mgñ*â-dharmas, see Sacred Books of the East, vol. xlix, p. 117.

Thought and Language Inseparable.

The theory of thought and language being inseparable which we find springing up independently in India, in Greece, and carried out to its last consequences by the Alexandrian Fathers of the Christian Church, has at last been recognised by modern philosophers also. When I brought it forward some years ago in my book 'On the Science of Thought,' it was treated at first as a mere paradox, as something new, and unheard of. The only profitable objection raised against my theory was that, as in our phenomenal world, that is, in space and time, no two things can ever be identical; neither could language and thought. But if that is the meaning of identical, it would follow that the word *identical* should be erased altogether from our dictionary, because no two things can ever be identical. My best critics knew better. They knew that I only wanted to prove once more what had been proved long ago by Greek and Indian philosophers, namely, that language and thought are one, and that in that sense the creative thoughts of the Supreme Being were called the logoi, and, if conceived as one, the Logos of God. It was the same Logos that was called by Philo and others, long before St. John, the *υἱὸς μονογενής* (Theosophy, p. 412), that is, the only begotten Son of God, in the sense of the first ideal creation or manifestation of the Godhead.

Coincidences between the Nâma-rûpa and the Greek Logos.

I must confess that when I met for the first time with this theory of the Supreme Being meditating on words, and shaping the world by means of words, I suspected more than a coincidence, I suspected a real influx of Greek thought into India. We are familiar with this theory from the Stoics and Neoplatonists, and we know in Greece the long antecedent historical development which led to it. We feel quite certain, therefore, that the Greeks could not have borrowed it from India, just as we can have no doubt that the idea of the Logos, and the very term of *υἱὸς μονογενής*—wrongly translated by *unigenitus* and only begotten—reached the Jews, like Philo, and the early Christians, like St. John, from the Greek schools at Alexandria. But a mere consideration of the dates of the texts in which the same thoughts, the theory of an ideal world, and of divine thoughts or words realised in the material world, are met with in India, renders all suspicion of borrowing impossible. And, after all, that theory that in the beginning there was the Word, or the words, and that by it or by them all things were made, is not so unnatural that it could not have sprung up independently in two places. The word is the manifestation of thought; every word, we must remember, expresses a concept, not a percept. Tree is not meant for this or that tree, it is the general concept of all trees; and if every individual thing is the realisation of an ideal type or thought or word, if every man, for instance, is the realisation of the divine thought or word of man, or of manhood, we need not be startled when we find in India as well as in Greece a belief that God created the world by the Logos or by the word, or by the many words, the logoi, the ideas of Plato, the species or types of modern science.

Speech as a Creative Power in the Veda.

The only surprising thing is that in the Vedic literature we should find, if not exactly the same, at least very much the same ideas, implied from the earliest times, and accepted without any attempt at explaining them. We can hardly account for this, unless we extend the period of the childhood of the Vedic people far beyond the date of their first poetical compositions. Thus we find in the Rig-veda a hymn placed in the mouth of Vâ*k* or Speech, which is unintelligible unless we admit a long previous growth of thought during which Speech had become not only one of many deities, but a kind of power even beyond the gods, a kind of Logos or primeval Wisdom. There Speech says of herself:

'I move along with Rudra, the god of storm and thunder, with the Vasus, with the Âdityas, with the Vi*s*ve Devas, I support both Mitra and Varu*n*a, the two A*s*vins, Indra and Agni.'

Now what can be the meaning of Speech supporting the greatest among the Vedic gods, unless she was conceived as a power greater than the gods?

Then she says again:

3. 'I am the Queen, the gatherer of treasures, I am intelligent, the first of those who deserve sacrifice; the gods have made me manifold, standing in many places, entering into many things.'

6. 'I stretch the bow for Rudra to kill the enemy, the hater of Brahman; I cause war for men, I stretch out heaven and earth.'

8. 'I breathe like the wind, holding to all things; beyond the sky, beyond this earth; such a one am I by my power.'

It does not seem to me that all this could be said, if Vâ*k* or Speech had been conceived simply as spoken language, or even as prayer or hymn of praise. It is quite true that from a very early time miraculous power was ascribed to the hymns of the Veda, whether for blessing or cursing. Still all this would not account for Vâ*k* or Speech stretching out heaven and earth, nay being greater than heaven and earth. Such expressions seem to me to presuppose in a distant past the conception of Speech or the Word as a creative power, though possibly in the vague character of the Jewish Wisdom (*Sophia*) rather than in the more definite form of the Greek *Logos.*

Similarity with the Old Testament Wisdom.

When we come to the Brâhma*n*as, we find there also many passages which would become far more intelligible, if we might take Vâ*k* or Speech in the sense of the Jewish Wisdom, who says (Prov. viii. 22), 'The Lord possessed me in the beginning of his way, before his works of old.'

23. 'I was set up from everlasting, from the beginning, or ever the earth was.'

25. 'Before the mountains were settled, before the hills was I brought forth.'

27. 'When he prepared the heavens, I was there; when he set a compass upon the face of the depth;'

30. 'Then I was by him, as one brought up with him, and I was daily his delight, rejoicing always before him.'

A very similar strain of thought meets us, for instance, in the Pa*ñk*avi*m*sa Brâhma*n*a XX, 14

2[1], where we read: 'Pragâpati, the Creator, was all this. He had Speech (vâ*k*) as his own, as a second, or in the language of the Bible, as one brought up with him. He thought, Let me send forth this speech; she will traverse and pervade all this. He sent her forth, and she traversed and pervaded all this.' In other passages vâ*k* is called the daughter, in others again the wife of the Creator or Pragâpati (as she is called his daily delight in the Old Testament), and she is always the principal agent in the work of creation. We read that 'all was made by vâ*k*, and likewise that all that was made, was vâ*k*' (*S*at. Br. VIII, 1, 2, 9; XI, 1, 6, 18; cf. Weber, Ind. Stud. x, p. 479). Just as we read in St. John, 'All things were made by the Word, and without the Word was not anything made that was made.'

Did Brahman mean Word?

That the ancient philosophers of India believed that the world was created by the Word, or that

[1] See Muir, Sanskrit Texts, v, p. 392.

in the beginning there was the Word, would become still more manifest, if we could prove that brahman had originally, long even before the composition of the Vedas, the meaning of word. Now there are passages in the Brâhma*n*as when it really seems as if we ought to translate brahman by *Word*, or when at all events the whole passage would become more intelligible if we did so. For instance, in the *S*atapatha Brâhma*n*a VI, 1, 1, 9 we read: 'Pra*g*âpati, the Lord of all created things, desired, "May I be more than one, may I be reproduced . . . He created first of all brahman."' Here I think that brahman was originally understood in the sense of Word, for immediately afterwards vâ*k*, Speech, takes the place of brahman, and from it everything else is produced. I should therefore translate, 'He created first of all the Word,' from which everything else proceeded. In later times this Word was identified with the Veda, nay even with the three Sa*m*hitâs, as we possess them, but this could hardly have been its original purport, though in our passage brahman is explained by 'the threefold Science,' that is, the threefold Veda.

This original meaning of brahman may afterwards have been forgotten, but we can discover faint traces of it here and there. Thus B*ri*has-pati, the lord of speech, is also called Vâ*k*as-pati, showing that b*ri*h and vâ*k* had the same meaning. Nay, the two, B*ri*has-pati and Vâ*k*, seem sometimes to form one deity (*S*atapath. Br. V, 3, 3, 5). Again in the *Kh*ând. Up. I, 3, 11, the B*ri*hatî, which is derived from b*ri*h, is explained by speech. Now this b*ri*h is the root from which brahman also is derived. If b*ri*h meant originally to break or burst forth, brahman would have meant at first what breaks forth, an utterance, a word, and in this sense and in the sense of prayer brahman is of very frequent occurrence in the Veda. It might, however, at the same time have meant what bursts forth in the sense of creation or creator, particularly when creation was conceived not as a making, but as a coming forth.

Brahman derived from the same Root as Verbum and Word.

We must now go a step further. The root b*ri*h exists also as b*ri*dh or v*ri*dh, and then means to burst forth, in the sense of growing. If then from v*ri*dh we formed a substantive vardha, this would in Latin regularly take the form of *verbum.* Latin has no dh, but represents dh by *f* or *b*, so that instead of Sanskrit rudhira, red, we have in Latin either *rufus* or *ruber*, in English *red.* And this takes us another step forward. As the Sanskrit dh is represented in English by d, this vardha, this Latin *verbum*, would regularly be reproduced in English by *word*, that is brahman, *verbum*, and *word* would all proceed from the same root v*ri*h or v*ri*dh, to burst forth, and would share the same meaning, viz. word. We must not conclude at once that therefore Brahman, as the source of the universe, was from the first conceived as the creative Word or the Logos. That would be too good to be true. But the fact that the same word brahman meant the creative power which bursts forth, and also the word that bursts forth, may have helped the earliest thinkers in India to the idea that the first bursting forth of the world was the word or thought uttered in and by Brahman.

Nâma-rûpa the Connecting-link between Brahman and the World.

There are other passages in the Brâhma*n*as which make it quite clear that the idea of a communication between the Creator and the created world by means of words was familiar to the Brâhmans at a very early time, though it was afterwards misunderstood and forgotten. Thus, as Professor Deussen pointed out, we read in the *S*atapatha Brâhma*n*a XI, 2, 3: 'Brahman was all this in the beginning. It sent forth (created) the gods, and having sent them forth, it established them over these worlds, Agni (fire) over the earth, Vâyu (wind) over the air, and Sûrya (sun) over the sky.' This is one visible world, but above this comes a higher world, and thus the Brâhma*n*a continues: 'As to the worlds above these, Brahman established over them the deities who are above the former deities. And as those worlds are manifest and their deities, these worlds also and their deities are manifest where he established them.' This gives us two worlds, but Brahman himself transcends them both. For the Brâhma*n*a continues:—'Then Brahman went to the half (which was not manifest) beyond, and having gone there, he thought, "How can I get into these worlds?" This shows that Brahman had been raised to so transcendent a height that he could no longer communicate with the real world. Still a communication was wanted, and how was it achieved? We are told, "*By words and forms*," that is by what the Stoics would have called the logoi or the logos. And thus we read, "And Brahman got into the worlds, by two, by forms (rûpa) and words (nâma). Of whatever thing there is a name, that is thus named; and of whatever thing there is no name, what one knows by form, saying it is such, that is such (of such form). For all this (universe) extends as far as name and form extend. These two, name and form, are the two great powers of Brahman, and whoever knows these two great powers of Brahman, becomes himself a great power. These are the two great revelations of Brahman, and whoever knows these two great revelations of Brahman, becomes himself a great revelation.'

In reading these scattered passages, it is difficult to resist the feeling that there is more behind them than the authors of the Brâhma*n*as themselves understood. Bráhman is conceived as sublimely transcendent, as not only above earth, air, and sky, but as beyond a second world which lies beyond this visible world. And if it was asked how this transcendent power could be brought into any relation with his own creation, the answer is by means of his two great powers and revelations, by means of words and forms, that is by means of those forms or εἴδη which are words, and by means of those words or λόγοι which are forms.

These are magnificent intuitions of truth, but they are almost beyond the intellectual reach of the authors of the Brâhma*n*as; they are like stars that have set beneath their horizon, and of which the later thinkers have caught but a faint glimmering here and there.

There is one more passage, perhaps the most decided, which has not yet been considered in connexion with this conception of Language and Reason as a creative power, and as a power for sustaining and pervading the world. It occurs in the Maitrâya*n*a Upanishad VI, 22, where we read: 'Two Brahmans have to be meditated on, the word and the non-word. By the word alone is the non-word revealed.' Here we have again the exact counterpart of the Logos of the Alexandrian schools. There is, according to the Alexandrian philosopher, the Divine Essence which is revealed by the Word, and the Word which alone reveals it. In its unrevealed state it is unknown, and was by some Christian philosophers called the Father; in its revealed state it was the Divine Logos or the Son.

From all this it seems to me that we are driven to admit that the same line of thought which, after a long preparation, found its final expression in Philo and later on in Clement of Alexandria, was worked out in India at a much earlier time, starting from very similar beginnings and arriving at very similar results. But there is nothing to indicate a borrowing on one side or the other.

The Gods of other Religions.

When the Vedântists have to deal with the gods of other religions, they naturally see in them, not their absolute Bráhman, but their qualified and active Brahmán, their Pragâpati, the Lord or Îsvara of all created things, their own Creator, Supporter, and Ruler of the world. Their language gives them a great advantage, for by a mere change of accent they can change the neuter Bráhman, with the accent on the first syllable, into the masculine Brahmán, with the accent on the last syllable. It is by these apparently insignificant contrivances that language may be said to help or to hinder thought. If we consider that by this masculine Brahmán they meant the active personal deity, endowed with all divine qualities, such as omnipotence, omniscience, justice, pity, and all the rest, it is easy to understand that such Deities as Jehovah, as represented in the Old Testament, and the Jehovah, or God the Father, as conceived in many passages of the New Testament, the Allâh of the Korân also, should have been identified by them with the masculine, not with the neuter Brahman. Nor did they thereby assign to these deities an inferior position. For their own phenomenal god, their Pragâpati or masculine Brahmán, though phenomenal, or as we might say, historical, was to them as real as anything, when known by us, can be. Nevertheless, behind that God, as known and named by human beings, they admitted an unknown God, or a Divine Nature, of which Pragâpati, Jehovah, Allâh, and God the Father would be the *personae* only. These personal aspects of the Divine Nature were meant for the human understanding and for human worship; they may be called historical, if only we remember that the history of God can only be the history of the human consciousness of God, or of the ideas which man, from the lowest stage of nature-worship to the highest stage of conscious divine sonship, has framed to himself of that transcendent Power which he feels both without and within. You will find that this concept of a Divine Nature in which the divine persons participate was familiar, not only to mediaeval Mystics, but to some of the most orthodox theologians also. Of course in the Middle Ages what was orthodox in one century became often unorthodox in the next, one Council condemned another, one Pope anathemised another. But the idea that there was a *Divina Essentia*, which was manifested in the

Father, the Son, and the Holy Ghost, was familiar to many Christian theologians, in ancient and modern times. Hence arose the danger on one side of substituting a Quaternity for the Trinity, that is the Divine Essence and the three substances, Father, Son, and Holy Ghost, or on the other side of changing the Trinity into three gods, distinct substantially, which would have been condemned as Tritheism [1].

While therefore the active deities of other religions were naturally recognised by modern followers of the Vedânta in their masculine Brahmán, the Divine Substance in which these gods participated, the Godhead which the Christian nominalists defined as a name common to the

[1] Nos (scil. Papa) sacro et universali concilio approbante credimus et confitemur cum Petro (Lombardo) quod una quaedam summa res est, incomprehensibilis quidem et ineffabilis, quae veraciter est pater et filius et spiritus, tres simul personae, ac singulatim quaelibet earundem. Et ideo in deo trinitas est solummodo, non quaternitas, quia quaelibet trium personarum est illa res, videlicet substantia, essentia, sivi natura divina, quae sola est universorum principium, praeter quod aliud inveniri non potest. See Harnack, Dogmengeschichte, iv, p. 447, note; Hagenbach, Dogmengeschichte, § 170, notes.

three persons, seemed to them to correspond best with the neuter Bráhman, the unknown, inconceivable, and ineffable God.

Nâma-rûpe, the Product of Avidyâ.

With all the similarities between Indian and European philosophy, however, there is, as there always will be, a difference, and a great difference.

First of all, these Nâma-rûpe, these logoi or the Logos, which could be represented as embodied in the Divine Wisdom in the West, remained with the Vedânta philosophers the result of Nescience, or Avidyâ. They were the thoughts of Brahmán, not of Bráhman, they belonged to the active and creative Brahmán, the Îsvara or Lord Such speculations are apt to make us feel giddy, but whatever we may think about them, they show at all events to what a height Indian philosophy had risen in its patient climb from peak to peak, and how strong its lungs must have been to be able to breathe in such an atmosphere.

Secondly, we must remember that what we call the creation of the world, as an historical act performed once, at a certain time, does not exist for the Vedântists. They speak of a repeated manifestation or coming forth from Brahmán, which had no beginning and will have no end. At the conclusion of great periods the universe is taken back into Brahmán and then sent forth again. But there never was a beginning and there never will be an end. There is an unbroken continuity between great periods or Kalpas, the work done in one continues to act in the next period, and that continuity rests on Brahmán, as the active and personal Lord (Î*s*vara). He sees that the next world should be what it ought to be, and that nothing should be lost. In some places certain latent powers or *s*aktis are ascribed to this Brahmán in order to account for the variety of created things in each period, for what we should call the various logoi or species. But this is strongly objected to by *S*aṅkara, who holds that the universe, though it has all its reality in and from Brahman, is not to be looked upon as a modification, or what, in these days, we should call evolution (pari*n*âma). For Bráhman, being perfect, can never be changed or modified, and what is called the created world in all its variety is and remains with the Vedântist the result of a primeval and universal turning aside or perversion (vivarta), caused by Avidyâ or Nescience. Hence the Creator as well as the creation, as such, possesses a relative reality only, or, as we should say, they are both phenomenal, just as every individual soul, as such, can claim no absolute reality, but remains phenomenal to itself till it has discovered its absolute reality in Bráhman which is hidden in every soul. Nay, as the individual soul has been made individual by means of the Upâdhis, the obstructions, i. e. the body, the senses, and the mind, the Creator also is what He is by means of the same Upâdhis, only Upâdhis of a much purer character (visuddha). This Creator or personal God, we should remember, is as real as our own personal self—and what can be more real in the ordinary language of the world? What seems unreasonable is that those who speak in the name of what they call common sense, should first deny that there can be any reality beyond that which we see and touch, and then protest if that higher reality in which they themselves do not believe is denied to the objects of their senses, and to all knowledge derived from them.

The Vedânta in Practical Life.

For all practical purposes, the Vedântist would hold that the whole phenomenal world, both in its objective and subjective character, should be accepted as real. It is as real as anything can be to the ordinary mind. It is not mere emptiness, as the Buddhists maintain. And thus the Vedânta philosophy leaves to every man a wide sphere of real usefulness, and places him under a law as strict and binding as anything can be in this transitory life. It leaves him a deity to worship as omnipotent and majestic as the deities of any other religions. It has room for almost every religion, nay, it embraces them all. Even when the higher light appears, that higher light does not destroy the reality of the former world, but imparts to it, even in its transitory and evanescent character, a fuller reality and a deeper meaning. Kant also knew that our world is and can be phenomenal only, and that the Ding an sich, in one sense the Bráhman, lies beyond our knowledge, that is, is separated from us by

Nescience, or Avidyâ, and he establishes his practical and moral philosophy for the phenomenal world, as if no noumenal world existed. Yet he retains the idea of a moral law for the phenomenal world in which we live, nay, he uses the idea of a moral law as the only certain proof of the existence of God. The Vedântist has an advantage of which he does not fail to avail himself. As the moral law is based on the Veda (Karmakâ*nd*a), he stands up for it as revealed truth for those who are still under the law, and he grants freedom to those only who are no longer of this world.

The Ethics of the Vedânta.

It has often been said that a philosophical religion like the Vedânta is deficient, because it cannot supply a solid foundation for morality. It is quite true that some philosophers hold that *ethics* have nothing to do with religion, and should have their own foundation, independent of all religion, though binding on every human being, whatever his religion may be. But this question, which is at present being agitated in the leading philosophical journals of Germany, France, and America, need not detain us, for I hope to be able to show that the Vedânta philosophy, so far from merely supplying a metaphysical explanation of the world, aims at establishing its ethics on the most solid philosophical and religious foundations.

I pointed out already that a very strict moral discipline is laid on everybody before he is even allowed to approach the study of the Vedânta, and that all authorities teach that no one could possibly enter into its spirit who has not previously subdued the passions and ambitions of the human heart. But there is still more in store to impart to this fleeting life a permanent moral purpose. You may remember that the Vedântists do not hold that the world was created at a certain time and once only, but that they consider the world eternal, only from time to time taken back into Brahmán and then emitted again from Brahmán. What we should call the active power in this process is the qualified Brahmán, the Lord (Îsvara), or, as we should say, the Creator of the world as it exists for us. But, if so, and if that Creator must be accepted as perfect, as just and righteous, how, we should ask with the Vedântist, can we ascribe to Him the wrongs with which the world abounds, and the apparently undeserved sufferings of its inhabitants? Why was one child born blind or brought up in a society where its moral nature must suffer shipwreck? Why are the bad so often triumphant, and the good trampled under foot? Why is there so much suffering at childbirth and at the approach of death? Why are the innocent punished, while the wicked escape? Various answers have been given to these questions by various philosophers and religious teachers. We may acquiesce in them, if we hold certain religious beliefs, but no system of pure ethics has been able to satisfy those who ask these questions in the agony of their undeserved afflictions. The answer of the Vedânta philosophers is well known, and has become the keynote not only of the Brâhmanic, but likewise of Buddhist morality, over the greater part of the world. There must be a cause, they say, to account for the effect which we see but too clearly, and that cause cannot possibly be found in the mere caprice or injustice of the Creator.

The Doctrine of Karman.

Therefore, if it is a result for us, it can only be the result of acts done in a former life. You see that the previous, nay the eternal existence of individual souls is taken for granted, as it seems to be likewise in certain passages of the New Testament (St. John ix). But whatever we may think of the premisses on which this theory rests, its influence on human character has been marvellous. If a man feels that what, without any fault of his own, he suffers in this life can only be the result of some of his own former acts, he will bear his sufferings with more resignation, like a debtor who is paying off an old debt. And if he knows besides that in this life he may by suffering not only pay off his old debts, but actually lay by moral capital for the future, he has a motive for goodness, which is not more selfish than it ought to be. The belief that no act, whether good or bad, can be lost, is only the same belief in the moral world which our belief in the preservation of force is in the physical world. Nothing can be lost. But while the Buddhists have accepted this ethical and metaphysical doctrine in its purely mechanical sense, as a belief in a power which acts without any divine superintendence, the Vedântists, who hold that the seeds of the world lie dormant in Brahmán during the interval between one age (kalpa) and another, between one creation and the next, teach that the effects which our past works will produce, depend after all on the creator and ruler of the world, the more or less personal Î*s*vara or Lord. Speaking, as they always do, in metaphors, they say that though the seeds of good and evil deeds are of our own sowing, their growth in the next world depends on the Lord, just as the growth of natural seeds depends on the rain and sunshine of heaven. However sceptical we may be on the power of any ethical teaching, and its influence on the practical conduct of men and women, there can be no doubt that this doctrine of Karman (karman means simply act or deed) has met with the widest acceptance, and has helped to soften the sufferings of millions, and to encourage them not only in their endurance of present evils, but likewise in their efforts to improve their future condition.

Pre-existence of the Soul.

One point is sometimes left in the dark, namely, how it is that we, who have no recollection of what we did in a former life, nay, who know nothing of that former life beyond its mere existence, should nevertheless be made to suffer for our former deeds or misdeeds. But why should we remember our former life, if we do not even remember the first two, three, or four years of our present life? The belief expressed by Wordsworth that

> 'The soul that rises with us, our life's star,
> Has had elsewhere its setting
> And cometh from afar,'

is possibly by this time a general belief; but the belief which is based on it, that our star in this life is what we made it in a former life, would probably sound strange, as yet, to many ears. Now it seems as if some teachers of the Vedânta had felt that the Karman, or the acts for which we suffer in this life or for which we are rewarded, need not have been exclusively those performed by ourselves, but that the Karman may be of a more collective character, and that as we enjoy so many of the rewards of good work done by others, we may also have to bear the consequences of evil deeds done by others. This would lead to the conception of the human race as one body or one family in which the whole suffers when any individual member suffers, for we are members one of another; it would account for the working of heredity or the perpetuation of acquired habits; nay, it would make us understand the meaning of the iniquity of the fathers being visited upon the children unto the third and fourth generation.

With the Vedântists this feeling of a common interest, nay, of the oneness or solidarity of the human race, was most natural. Their whole philosophy was built on the conviction that every human being has its true being in Bráhman, and this feeling, though it is chiefly metaphysical, breaks out occasionally as a moral power also. We say, We should love our neighbour as ourselves. The Vedântist says, We should love our neighbours as our self, that is, we should love them not for what is merely phenomenal in them, for their goodness, or beauty, or strength, or kindness, but for their soul, for the divine Self in all of them. Thus, in the Upanishads, an old sage, who takes leave of his two wives when retiring into the forest, says to his beloved Maitrêyi (B*ri*h. Âr. II, 4): 'Thou who art truly dear to me, thou speakest dear words. Come, sit down, I will explain it to thee, and mark well what I say. And he said: "Verily, a husband is not dear, that you may love the husband; but that you may love the Self, therefore a husband is dear. Verily, a wife is not dear, that you may love the wife; but that you may love the Self, therefore a wife is dear."'

This is carried on to sons, and friends, to the gods and all creatures, they all are to be loved, not for themselves as they appear, but for the Self that is in them, for their eternal Self, for that universal Self in which we all share, in which we all live and move and have our being. Like many a truth in Eastern religion, this truth also, that in loving our neighbour we really love God, and that in loving our neighbour we love ourselves, has sometimes been carried to an extreme, till it became a caricature. But, nevertheless, it shows an enormous amount of intellectual labour to have reasoned out that we should love our neighbour, because in loving him we love God, and in loving God, we love ourselves. The deep truth that lies hidden in this, was certainly not elaborated by any other nation, so far as I know.

So much to show that the Vedânta philosophy, abstruse as its metaphysics are, has not neglected the important sphere of Ethics, but that on the contrary, we find ethics in the beginning, ethics in the middle, and ethics in the end, to say nothing of the fact that minds so engrossed with divine things as the Vedânta philosophers, are not likely to fall victims to the ordinary temptations of the world, the flesh, and other powers.

Recapitulation.

I wish that you should carry away a clear idea of the Vedânta philosophy, if not in all its details—that is impossible—but at least in its general purpose. It is a very bad habit to say, 'Oh, philosophy is too deep for me,' or to dispose of

Eastern philosophy by saying that it is esoteric or mystic. Remember that all this Vedânta philosophy was never esoteric, but that it was open to all, and was elaborated by men who, in culture and general knowledge, stood far below any one of us here present. Should we not be able to follow in their footsteps? Should the wisdom reached by the dark-skinned inhabitants of India two or three thousand years ago be too high or too deep for us? And as to their philosophy being called *mystic*, it really seems to me as if those who are so fond of using that name, spell it, perhaps, with an 'i,' and not with a 'y.' They seem to imagine that mystic philosophy must be full of mist and clouds and vapour. True mystic philosophy, however, is as clear as a summer sky, it is full of brightness and full of warmth. Mystic meant originally no more than what required preparation and initiation, and mysteries were not dark things left dark, but dark things made bright and clear and intelligible.

If a system of philosophy is a consistent, and, as it were, an organic whole, springing from one small seed, it should always be possible to fix on its central truth from which all its dogmas proceed, and, leaving out all bywork and ornamentation, to trace the direction in which its arguments move, and to discover the goal which they are meant to reach.

Now, the quintessence of the Vedânta philosophy has been well formulated by a native philosopher in one short line, and it would be well if the same could be done for other systems of philosophy also. Our Vedântist says:

श्लोकार्धेन प्रवक्ष्यामि यदुक्तं ग्रंथकोटिभिः ।
ब्रह्म सत्यं जगन्मिथ्या जीवो ब्रह्मैव नापरः ॥

'In one half verse I shall tell you what has been told in thousands of volumes:—Brahman is true, the world is false, man's soul is Brahman and nothing else'—or, as we should say: 'God is true, the world is fleeting, man's soul is God and nothing else.' And then he adds:—

यल्लाभान्नापरो लाभः यत्सुखान्नापरं सुखं ।
यज्ज्ञानान्नापरं ज्ञानं तद्ब्रह्मेत्यवधारयेत् ॥

'There is nothing worth gaining, there is nothing worth enjoying, there is nothing worth knowing but Brahman alone; for he who *knows* Brahman, *is* Brahman.' This, too, we might possibly translate by the more familiar words: 'What shall it profit a man, if he shall gain the whole world, and lose his own soul?'

THE END.